Soup *to* Nuts

President: Thomas F. McDow III
Vice-President: Dave Kempf
Managing Editor: Mary Cummings
Project Manager: Tanis Westbrook
Essayist: Carolyn King
Art Director: Steve Newman
Book Design: Bill Kersey
Cover Design: Jim Scott
Typographers: Jessie Anglin, Sara Anglin
Production: Mark Sloan
Production Coordinator: Powell Ropp

Soup to Nuts
is a collection of our favorite recipes,
which are not necessarily original recipes.

Published by
Favorite Recipes® Press
an imprint of FRP

FRP™

P.O. Box 305142
Nashville, Tennessee 37230

Manufactured in the United States of America
First Printing 2001 24,000 copies

Contents

Introduction

 From soup to nuts—a phrase meaning that which is all-inclusive, an idiom grounded in food terminology that has become generic in its applications. A to Z; everything but the kitchen sink; alpha to omega. But, in a nutshell, what is the origin of the saying? There's speculation: likely it refers to multicourse meals that began with soup and were topped off with a serving of nuts. However, talk to any group of people and you'll find those who have heard the expression all their lives and those for whom it is entirely new. It's nothing that can be pinned down, though: those who have heard it forever have no idea where it originated. Is it regional? Is it generational? If searching out lingual origins is just your cup of soup, and you have a few ideas, we'd like to hear from you.

Soup, from the Latin *suppa*, is basically water or liquid in which all manner of solid foods have been cooked. It's a comfort food, and as soup is a mishmash of favorite ingredients, so our book is a hodgepodge of soups and other favorite foods to make your culinary life a comfort. Bouillabaisse, goulash, bisques, stews, chowders, chilies, gumbo, melon soup—how we vary our soups seems endless, and in our soups section you're sure to find recipes to suit your inclination.

You're just as sure to find tempting ways to prepare nut-based dishes in our chapter devoted exclusively to the nut. Defined as fruits with woody outer casings and soft edible skins enclosing edible kernels, nuts have been a food source from earliest times. Used in extracts, pastes, butters, and oils, nuts play a prominent and versatile role in cookery as well as in everyday practical necessities, such as soaps and inks.

In our book, the distance from soup to nuts is separated by appetizers, salads, entrées, side dishes, breads, and desserts, although technically, there may be no distance at all between the two, as with a soup sprinkled with toasted almond slivers. Whatever the category, from *Soup to Nuts* is a passage through a great many pages of recipes you won't want to miss. Enjoy the journey.

Soups
Appetizers
Salads

Bean and Tomato Soup

1 (16-ounce) can stewed tomatoes, chopped
1/2 cup ground cooked ham
1 (24-ounce) jar Great Northern beans

*Combine undrained tomatoes, ham and beans in large
microwave-safe bowl. Microwave on High until heated through,
stirring once. Serve with corn bread or fruit muffins.*
Yield: 4 servings.

Creole Beef Stew

3 tablespoons flour
1/2 teaspoon ground ginger
1 teaspoon salt
1/2 teaspoon celery salt
1/4 teaspoon garlic salt
1/4 teaspoon pepper
3 pounds chuck roast, cut into 2-inch cubes
2 tablespoons shortening or bacon drippings
1 (16-ounce) can tomatoes
3 medium onions, sliced
1/3 cup red wine vinegar
1/2 cup molasses
6 to 8 carrots, sliced diagonally 1 inch thick
1/2 cup raisins

*Mix flour, ginger, salt, celery salt, garlic salt and pepper together. Toss with
beef cubes, coating well. Brown beef cubes in shortening in large heavy
saucepan. Add tomatoes, onions, vinegar and molasses; mix well. Bring to a
boil; reduce heat. Simmer, covered, for 2 hours. Add carrots
and raisins. Simmer for 30 minutes or until carrots are tender.*
Yield: 8 to 10 servings.

*Shelled nuts should
be stored in the
refrigerator or freezer.
Because of their high
fat content, they tend
to become rancid if
kept at room
temperature too long.*

French Onion Soup

2 cups melted butter or margarine
16 to 18 onions, thinly sliced
8 (10-ounce) cans beef consommé
2 consommé cans water
12 slices toasted French bread
1 cup (or more) grated Parmesan cheese

Heat large baking dish in oven until hot. Combine butter, onions and 1 can consommé in large saucepan. Cook until onions are tender, but not brown, stirring frequently. Spoon into heated baking dish. Bring remaining consommé and water to a boil in saucepan. Pour over onions. Top with bread; sprinkle with cheese. Broil until cheese is light brown. Ladle into soup bowls.
Yield: 12 servings.

Garden Gazpacho with White Beans

4 plum tomatoes, cored, chopped
1 small onion, chopped
1 green or red bell pepper, chopped
1 cucumber, peeled, chopped
1 small jalapeño, seeded, minced
2 cloves of garlic, minced
2 tablespoons minced fresh basil
1½ teaspoons ground cumin
1 teaspoon hot pepper sauce
¼ teaspoon salt
¼ teaspoon pepper
1½ cups navy beans or small white beans
2 cups canned tomato juice

Combine tomatoes, onion, bell pepper, cucumber, jalapeño, garlic, basil, cumin, hot pepper sauce, salt and pepper in food processor container. Process for 10 to 15 seconds or until mashed. Pour into large bowl. Stir in beans and tomato juice. Chill for 1 hour or longer.
Yield: 4 servings.

Taco-in-a-Bowl

1½ pounds lean ground beef
1 large onion, chopped
1 (28-ounce) can crushed tomatoes in purée
1 (15-ounce) can kidney beans
1 envelope taco seasoning mix
1 (8-ounce) can corn
1 small avocado, chopped
¼ cup sliced black olives

*Brown ground beef with onion in saucepan, stirring frequently; drain.
Add tomatoes, undrained beans, seasoning mix and undrained corn;
mix well. Simmer for 15 minutes, adding tomato juice if necessary for desired
consistency. Add avocado and olives. Cook just until heated through.
Ladle into soup bowls. Garnish servings with sour cream. Serve with
shredded Cheddar cheese and tortilla chips.
Yield: 4 to 6 servings.*

Chilled Zucchini Soup

3 medium zucchini, sliced
3 ribs celery, sliced
2 green onions with tops, sliced
1 carrot, peeled, sliced ▪ 1 clove of garlic, minced
1 teaspoon chopped parsley
½ teaspoon dillweed
¼ teaspoon thyme ▪ 1 teaspoon salt
¼ teaspoon pepper
6 cups chicken broth ▪ 1½ cups sour cream

*Combine zucchini, celery, green onions, carrot, garlic, parsley, ½ teaspoon
dillweed, thyme, salt, pepper and chicken broth in saucepan. Simmer for 10
minutes or until vegetables are tender-crisp. Reserve several slices vegetables in
bowl. Purée remaining vegetables and broth in blender. Add 1 cup sour cream;
process until smooth. Spoon into bowl with reserved vegetable slices.
Chill, covered, until thoroughly chilled. Spoon into serving bowls. Serve with
dollop of sour cream and sprinkle with additional dillweed.
Yield: 6 servings.*

Soups • Appetizers • Salads

Sparkling Limeade

1 large lime
$1/2$ cup sugar
$1^1/3$ cups water
2 cups club soda
Pinch of salt

Place lime, sugar and water in blender container. Process at high speed for 30 seconds. Strain liquid into pitcher. Add club soda and salt. Serve immediately. Yield: 3 servings.

Mint Tea

Peels of 3 lemons
6 cups water
2 cups sugar
$1^1/2$ teaspoons each almond and vanilla extract
Juice of 3 lemons
4 cups water
4 tea bags
2 (46-ounce) cans pineapple juice
Fresh mint to taste

Combine lemon peels, 6 cups water and sugar in saucepan. Boil for 5 minutes; discard lemon peels. Add flavorings and lemon juice. Bring 4 cups water to a boil in saucepan; remove from heat. Add tea bags. Steep for several minutes; discard tea bags. Add to the sugar syrup. Stir in pineapple juice. Pour into two 1-gallon containers. Chill until serving time. Serve over ice in glasses; add mint. May add ginger ale to taste to serve as a punch. Yield: 24 servings.

Bleu Cheese Crisps

8 ounces bleu cheese
4 ounces unsalted butter, softened
1 egg
1 teaspoon finely ground pepper
1/4 cup chopped pecans
1 3/4 cups flour

Cream bleu cheese and butter in bowl. Add egg, pepper, pecans and flour; mix well. Shape into two 1 1/2-inch-diameter rolls; wrap in waxed paper. Chill for 4 hours to overnight. Slice 1/4 inch thick; place on ungreased baking sheet. Bake at 425 degrees for 10 minutes or until light brown. Yield: 4 dozen.

Party Cheese Ball

8 ounces Cheddar cheese, grated
1 tablespoon finely chopped pimento
1 tablespoon finely chopped green bell pepper
1 tablespoon finely chopped onion
1/4 teaspoon salt
1 teaspoon Worcestershire sauce
1 cup chopped pecans
16 ounces cream cheese, softened

Combine Cheddar cheese, pimento, green pepper, onion, salt, Worcestershire sauce and 1/2 cup pecans in large bowl. Add cream cheese; mix well. Shape mixture into ball or log. Roll in remaining 1/2 cup pecans. Yield: 48 servings.

Soups • Appetizers • Salads

Microwave Crab Dip

16 ounces cream cheese, cubed, softened
1 clove of garlic
1 small onion, cut into quarters
$1/3$ cup mayonnaise
1 teaspoon sugar
Dash of salt
1 (6-ounce) can crab meat, drained, flaked
$1/4$ cup white grape juice

*Combine cream cheese, garlic, onion, mayonnaise, sugar and salt
in blender container. Process until smooth. Add crab meat. Process until
crab meat is chopped but not puréed. Spoon into glass dish. Microwave on
Medium for 5 minutes or until heated through. Stir in grape juice.
Serve with assorted crackers.
Yield: 20 servings.*

Black Bean Salsa

1 (15-ounce)) can black beans
1 cup hot salsa
$1/4$ cup chopped green onions
$1/4$ cup chopped red bell pepper
1 tablespoon lime juice
1 tablespoon olive oil
$1/2$ teaspoon minced garlic
$1/4$ teaspoon ground cumin
$1^1/2$ tablespoons chopped cilantro
1 ripe avocado

*Rinse black beans; drain. Combine with salsa, green onions, red pepper,
lime juice, olive oil, garlic, cumin and cilantro in bowl; mix well. Mash
avocado in bowl just before serving time. Stir avocado into black bean mixture.
Spoon into serving bowl. Serve with tortilla chips.
Yield: $4^1/2$ cups.*

*To determine if
pecans bought in
the shell are fresh,
shake them.
If the kernels inside
rattle, they are old
and dried out.*

Garden Greek Appetizer

8 ounces cream cheese, softened
8 ounces feta cheese, crumbled
1/4 cup plain yogurt
1 clove of garlic, minced
1/4 teaspoon pepper
2 tomatoes, seeded, chopped
1 medium seedless cucumber, chopped
3 green onions, finely chopped
3 black olives, finely chopped

Process cream cheese, feta cheese, yogurt, garlic and pepper in food processor until smooth. Spread cheese mixture in 10-inch pie plate. Chill until firm. Top with tomatoes, cucumber, green onions and black olives. Serve with mini pitas. Yield: 10 to 12 servings.

The Haystack

1 (16-ounce) can refried beans
1/2 envelope taco seasoning mix
Tabasco sauce to taste
1 ripe avocado, sliced
1 1/2 tablespoons lemon juice
1/2 cup sour cream
1 (4-ounce) can chopped green chiles, drained
1 (4-ounce) can chopped black olives
1/4 cup chopped green onions
3/4 cup shredded Monterey Jack cheese
3/4 cup shredded Cheddar cheese
1/2 cup chopped tomatoes
1 to 2 cups alfalfa sprouts

Combine refried beans, taco seasoning mix and Tabasco sauce in small bowl. Spread in 1/2-inch-thick circle in center of large platter. Beat avocado, lemon juice and sour cream in mixer bowl until smooth. Spread over bean mixture. Layer with green chiles, olives, green onions, cheeses and tomatoes, shaping into pyramid. Cover with alfalfa sprouts. Serve with corn or taco chips. Yield: 15 servings.

Fiesta Roll

2 (10-ounce) packages frozen chopped spinach, thawed
1 small envelope dry Hidden Valley ranch salad dressing mix
6 green onions, chopped
$\frac{1}{4}$ to $\frac{1}{2}$ cup bacon bits, crushed
1 cup mayonnaise
1 cup sour cream
10 large flour tortillas

*Squeeze spinach dry. Combine with salad dressing mix, onions,
bacon bits, mayonnaise and sour cream in bowl; mix well. Spread over
tortillas; roll as for jelly roll. Wrap in plastic wrap. Chill for several hours.
Cut into thin slices. Arrange on serving plate.
Yield: 60 servings.*

Fruited Canapés

8 ounces whipped cream cheese with pineapple
$\frac{1}{4}$ cup chutney
8 rectangles rye or wheat crisp bread, cut into halves
$\frac{1}{2}$ cup drained blueberries
$\frac{1}{2}$ cup drained sliced strawberries
$\frac{1}{2}$ cup drained mandarin oranges
$\frac{1}{4}$ cup confectioners' sugar

*Combine cream cheese and chutney in bowl; mix well. Spread on crisp bread.
Arrange fruit over cream cheese mixture. Sift confectioners' sugar over top.
Serve canapés immediately or chill, covered, for up to 1 hour.
Yield: 16 servings.*

Spinach and Cheese Puff Balls

1 (10-ounce) package frozen chopped spinach
1/2 cup chopped onion
2 eggs, lightly beaten
1/3 cup bleu cheese salad dressing
1/2 cup shredded Cheddar cheese
1/2 cup grated Parmesan cheese
2 tablespoons butter, melted
1/8 teaspoon garlic powder
Dijon mustard to taste
1 (8 1/2-ounce) package corn muffin mix

Cook spinach using package directions, adding onion; drain well and press dry. Combine eggs, salad dressing, cheeses, butter, garlic powder and mustard in bowl; mix well. Stir in spinach and muffin mix. Chill, covered, for 1 hour or until easy to handle. Shape into 1-inch balls; arrange on baking sheet. Chill, covered, until 20 minutes before serving. Bake at 350 degrees for 10 to 15 minutes or until light brown. Serve warm with mustard.
Yield: 50 puff balls.

Peanuts take up moisture easily. For maximum crispness, as in salads and sauces, don't add peanuts until just before serving.

Turkey Cranberry Croissants

8 ounces cream cheese, softened
1/4 cup orange marmalade
1/2 cup chopped pecans
6 croissants or rolls, split into halves
1 pound thinly sliced cooked turkey
3/4 cup whole cranberry sauce
Lettuce leaves

Combine cream cheese, marmalade and pecans in small bowl. Spread cream cheese mixture on both halves of croissants. Layer turkey, cranberry sauce and lettuce on half the croissants. Top with remaining croissant halves.
Yield: 6 servings.

Photograph for this recipe is on the cover.

Frosted Cranberry Salad

1/2 cup chopped pecans ▪ 1 tablespoon melted butter
1 (14-ounce) can crushed pineapple ▪ 2 (3-ounce) packages lemon gelatin
1 cup ginger ale ▪ 1 (16-ounce) can cranberry sauce
1 envelope whipped topping mix ▪ 8 ounces cream cheese, softened

*Combine pecans and butter on baking sheet. Bake in 350-degree oven until
light brown, stirring occasionally. Cool. Drain pineapple, reserving juice.
Combine reserved juice with enough water to measure 1 cup. Bring to a boil in
saucepan. Remove from heat. Add gelatin, stirring until dissolved. Cool. Stir in
ginger ale. Chill until partially set. Fold in mixture of pineapple and
cranberry sauce. Spoon into 9x9-inch dish. Chill until set. Prepare whipped
topping mix using package directions. Fold in cream cheese. Spread over
gelatin mixture; sprinkle with toasted pecans. Chill until serving time.
Yield: 12 servings.*

Orange Blossom Salad

1 (3-ounce) package lemon gelatin ▪ 1 1/2 cups boiling water
1/4 cup lemon juice ▪ 8 ounces cream cheese, softened
1 cup shredded Cheddar cheese ▪ 1/2 cup chopped pecans
1 (16-ounce) can pineapple chunks
2 (3-ounce) packages orange gelatin ▪ 2 cups ginger ale
2 (11-ounce) cans mandarin oranges, drained
Green or red grape clusters ▪ 1 egg white, beaten
Sugar or flavored gelatin ▪ Lettuce leaves

*Dissolve lemon gelatin in 1 1/2 cups boiling water in saucepan. Stir in lemon
juice. Add gradually to cream cheese in bowl, beating at medium speed until
smooth. Chill until partially set. Fold in Cheddar cheese and pecans. Spoon
into oiled 10-cup ring mold. Chill until almost set. Drain pineapple, reserving
juice. Add enough water to reserved juice to measure 1 1/2 cups. Bring to a boil
in saucepan. Stir in orange gelatin until dissolved; remove from heat. Add
ginger ale gradually. Chill until partially set. Fold in oranges and pineapple.
Spoon over congealed layer. Chill for 8 hours to overnight. Brush grape
clusters with egg white; sprinkle with sugar. Let stand on rack until dry.
Unmold salad onto lettuce-lined serving plate; garnish with grapes.
Yield: 12 servings.*

Pear and Walnut Salad

1/2 cup vegetable oil
3 tablespoons vinegar
1/4 cup sugar
1/2 teaspoon celery seeds
1/4 teaspoon salt
1/4 cup walnut halves
4 cups torn lettuce
1 pear, sliced or chopped
2 ounces bleu cheese, crumbled

*Combine oil, vinegar, sugar, celery seeds and salt in jar with tight-fitting lid;
shake to dissolve sugar and mix well. Chill in refrigerator. Spread walnuts in
baking dish. Bake at 375 degrees for 3 to 5 minutes or until golden brown,
stirring occasionally. Combine walnuts with lettuce, pear and bleu cheese in
salad bowl. Add dressing at serving time; toss lightly to coat well.*
Yield: 4 servings.

Quick Frozen Fruit Salad

8 ounces cream cheese, softened
2 cups sour cream
1 cup sugar
2 tablespoons lemon juice
2 teaspoons vanilla extract
12 ounces whipped topping
1 (16-ounce) can crushed pineapple, drained
2 large bananas, chopped
1 cup mixed candied fruit
1 cup chopped pecans

*Combine cream cheese, sour cream, sugar, lemon juice and vanilla in
mixer bowl; beat until smooth. Fold in whipped topping. Add
pineapple, bananas, candied fruit and pecans; mix gently. Spoon into
mold. Freeze until firm. Unmold onto serving plate.*
Yield: 16 servings.

Frozen Waldorf Salad

1 (9-ounce) can crushed pineapple
2 eggs, lightly beaten
1/2 cup sugar ▪ 1/4 cup lemon juice
1/8 teaspoon salt ▪ 1/4 cup mayonnaise
2 1/2 cups chopped unpeeled Red Delicious apples
2/3 cup diced celery
1/2 cup coarsely chopped walnuts
1/3 cup miniature marshmallows
1/2 cup whipping cream, whipped

Drain pineapple, reserving syrup. Combine syrup, eggs, sugar, lemon juice and salt in saucepan. Cook over low heat for 20 minutes or until slightly thickened, stirring constantly. Cool. Fold in mayonnaise. Combine pineapple, apples, celery, walnuts and marshmallows in bowl; mix well. Fold whipped cream into cooled egg mixture. Pour over fruit mixture; toss lightly. Spoon into paper-lined muffin cups. Freeze until firm. Place in refrigerator for 1 hour before serving. Remove paper liners from each salad; invert onto lettuce-lined serving plate.
Yield: 12 servings.

One ounce of whole shelled almonds contains 170 calories, 6 grams protein, 14 grams fat, 5 grams carbohydrate, and 4 milligrams of sodium.

Chicken Salad Galore

2 1/2 cups mayonnaise
1/2 cup sour cream ▪ 1 tablespoon curry powder
3 cups cold cooked rice
5 cups chopped cooked chicken breasts
1 1/2 cups chopped green bell pepper
3 cups chopped celery ▪ 3/4 cup seedless raisins
1 1/4 cups slivered almonds
3 (11-ounce) cans mandarin oranges, drained
2 (8-ounce) cans sliced water chestnuts, drained
Salt and pepper to taste

Combine mayonnaise, sour cream and curry powder in large bowl; mix well. Add rice, chicken, green pepper, celery, raisins, almonds, mandarin oranges, water chestnuts, salt and pepper; toss to mix well. Spoon into serving bowl.
Yield: 20 servings.

Chinese Chicken Salad

5 cups chopped cooked chicken
1 cup sliced water chestnuts
2 cups pineapple tidbits
2 cups mandarin oranges
1 cup chopped celery
$\frac{1}{2}$ cup sliced green onions
$\frac{1}{2}$ cup slivered almonds
Chicken Salad Dressing
2 (3-ounce) cans Chinese noodles

*Combine chicken, water chestnuts, pineapple, mandarin oranges, celery,
green onions and almonds in bowl. Add Chicken Salad Dressing; mix well. Chill
until serving time. Add noodles just before serving.
Yield: 10 to 12 servings.*

Chicken Salad Dressing

$\frac{1}{4}$ cup chutney
1 cup sour cream
1 cup mayonnaise
1 teaspoon (scant) curry powder

*Combine chutney, sour cream, mayonnaise and curry powder
in bowl; mix well. Chill in refrigerator until needed.
Yield: $2\frac{1}{4}$ cups.*

Soups • Appetizers • Salads

Almond Salad with Orange Vinaigrette

2 tablespoons melted butter
1 egg white, at room temperature
¼ cup sugar
1 cup sliced almonds
1 head Bibb lettuce, torn into bite-size pieces
1 head leaf lettuce, torn into bite-size pieces
1 (11-ounce) can mandarin oranges, drained
10 strawberries, thinly sliced
1 green onion, chopped
Orange Vinaigrette Dressing

Coat bottom of 9x9-inch baking pan with butter. Beat egg white in mixer bowl at high speed until foamy. Add sugar 1 tablespoon at a time, beating constantly until stiff peaks form. Fold in almonds. Spread mixture in prepared pan. Bake at 325 degrees for 20 to 25 minutes or until almonds are dry, stirring every 5 minutes. Cool. Combine Bibb lettuce, leaf lettuce, mandarin oranges, strawberries and green onion in bowl; mix well. Toss with Orange Vinaigrette Dressing. Spoon salad onto salad plates; sprinkle with almonds.
Yield: 6 servings.

Orange Vinaigrette Dressing

¾ cup olive oil
¼ cup red wine vinegar
1 tablespoon orange juice
1 teaspoon grated orange peel
½ teaspoon poppy seeds
⅛ teaspoon salt
⅛ teaspoon pepper

Whisk olive oil, wine vinegar, orange juice, orange peel, poppy seeds, salt and pepper in bowl until combined.
Yield: 1 cup.

Herbed Bean Salad

¼ cup lemon juice
¼ cup white wine vinegar
1 tablespoon Dijon mustard
1 tablespoon honey mustard
1 small clove of garlic, minced
1 tablespoon chopped fresh basil
1½ teaspoons chopped fresh thyme
½ teaspoon salt
⅛ teaspoon pepper
¼ cup olive oil or vegetable oil
3 cups small white beans
1 cup chopped seeded peeled cucumber
1 cup chopped red bell pepper
2 tablespoons chopped celery
2 tablespoons chopped green onions
2 tablespoons chopped parsley
4 to 8 ounces whole tender green beans, trimmed
6 cherry tomatoes, cut into halves

Combine lemon juice, vinegar, mustards, garlic, basil, thyme, salt and pepper in bowl and whisk until smooth. Whisk in olive oil gradually. Combine white beans, cucumber, bell pepper, celery, green onions and parsley in bowl. Add ½ cup dressing and toss to coat well. Let stand at room temperature for 1 hour. Steam green beans for 2 minutes or until tender-crisp; drain. Add 2 tablespoons dressing to warm beans. Arrange white bean mixture, green beans and tomatoes on lettuce-lined salad plates. Serve with remaining dressing. Yield: 6 servings.

Coleslaw

2 pounds cabbage, thinly sliced
1 green bell pepper, thinly sliced
1 red bell pepper, thinly sliced
1 medium sweet onion, thinly sliced
1 jalapeño, seeded, minced
1/2 teaspoon salt
Coleslaw Dressing
1/2 cup coarsely chopped dry-roasted peanuts

*Combine cabbage, bell peppers, onion, jalapeño and salt in bowl and
mix well. Chill in refrigerator. Add Coleslaw Dressing and toss to coat well.
Let stand for 2 hours. Add peanuts and toss gently.
Yield: 8 servings.*

Coleslaw Dressing

1/4 cup chunky peanut butter
1 tablespoon fresh lime juice
1 tablespoon grated gingerroot
2 teaspoons grated garlic
2 teaspoons sugar
1 teaspoon soy sauce
1/4 cup water

*Combine peanut butter, lime juice, gingerroot, garlic, sugar
and soy sauce in bowl and mix well. Whisk in water gradually.
Let stand at room temperature.
Yield: 1/2 cup.*

Health Salad

1 head Boston lettuce
1 small cucumber ▪ 2 small tomatoes
1 green bell pepper ▪ 5 radishes
1/2 avocado ▪ 1 peach
1 slice canned pineapple, drained
1/2 cup mandarin oranges, drained
8 ounces fresh strawberries
3 tablespoons corn oil ▪ 1 small onion, minced
2 teaspoons prepared mustard
6 tablespoons lemon juice
1/4 teaspoon salt ▪ 1/8 teaspoon pepper
1 sprig of parsley, chopped
1/2 teaspoon dried dillweed
1/4 teaspoon dried tarragon
1/4 teaspoon dried basil

Tear lettuce into bite-size pieces. Cut vegetables and fruits into bite-size pieces. Combine in large bowl. Mix oil, onion, mustard, lemon juice, salt, pepper, parsley, dillweed, tarragon and basil in small bowl. Pour over salad; mix gently. Marinate, covered, for 10 minutes. Serve in glass bowl.
Yield: 4 to 6 servings.

Bleu Cheese Potato Salad

8 medium potatoes, cooked, peeled, chopped
2 tablespoons chopped parsley
3 green onions with tops, chopped
4 ounces bleu cheese, crumbled
1/2 cup slivered almonds ▪ 3 hard-boiled eggs, chopped
1 cup sour cream ▪ 1/4 cup light vinegar
2 1/2 teaspoons salt
1/4 teaspoon pepper ▪ Paprika to taste

Combine potatoes with parsley, green onions, bleu cheese, almonds and eggs in large bowl. Add mixture of sour cream, vinegar, salt and pepper; mix gently. Sprinkle with paprika. Chill until serving time.
Yield: 12 servings.

Roasted Potato Salad

3 pounds red boiling potatoes
1/3 cup olive oil
1 clove of garlic
1/4 cup red wine vinegar
1 tablespoon fresh rosemary, or 1 teaspoon dried
Salt to taste
1/3 cup olive oil
2 pounds green beans, cut into 1-inch pieces
1 red onion
30 kalamata or niçoise olives, cut into halves

Cut unpeeled potatoes into halves and then into 1-inch wedges. Combine with 1/3 cup olive oil in large roasting pan, tossing to coat well. Roast at 450 degrees for 30 minutes or until tender, stirring every 10 minutes. Cool potatoes in pan. Process garlic, vinegar, rosemary, salt and 1/3 cup olive oil in blender until smooth. Cook beans in salted water in saucepan for 5 minutes or until tender-crisp; drain. Cut onion into halves lengthwise and then into thin slices. Crisp in ice water for 5 minutes; drain and pat dry. Combine potatoes, beans, onion, olives and dressing in bowl; toss lightly to coat well. Garnish with sprigs of fresh rosemary. Serve at room temperature.
Yield: 10 servings.

Blanch nuts by covering with rapidly boiling water and allowing to stand just until skins are loosened. Drain nuts and spread on paper towel to dry. Remove skins by squeezing between thumb and index finger. For best results, blanch only 1/2 cup nuts at a time and allow to stand in the water the shortest time possible.

Hawaiian Sweet Potato Salad

8 ounces bacon, cut into ½-inch pieces
3 cups cooked chopped sweet potatoes
2 cups pineapple chunks ▪ ½ cup mayonnaise
1 tablespoon Dijon mustard
2 tablespoons fresh lime juice ▪ ½ teaspoon pepper
½ cup chopped macadamia nuts
Lettuce leaves

Fry bacon in skillet until crisp; drain. Crumble bacon. Mix with sweet potatoes and pineapple in large bowl. Combine mayonnaise, Dijon mustard, lime juice and pepper in small bowl; mix well. Add to sweet potato mixture; mix gently. stir in nuts. Spoon into lettuce-lined serving bowl.
Yield: 4 to 6 servings.

Brown Rice and Vegetable Salad

1 cup brown rice
1 cup fresh green beans, strung, broken
¾ cup thinly sliced carrots
1 cup frozen green peas
1 red bell pepper, chopped
1 cucumber, peeled, seeded, chopped
1 large tomato, chopped
⅓ cup toasted unsalted sunflower kernels
1 cup shredded Monterey Jack cheese
¼ cup reduced-calorie Italian salad dressing
3 tablespoons tarragon vinegar
2 tablespoons virgin olive oil
⅓ teaspoon coarsely ground pepper

Cook rice using package directions; set aside in refrigerator. Boil green beans and carrots in saucepan until tender-crisp; drain and cool. Bring peas to a boil in saucepan; remove from heat immediately and drain. Mix with beans and carrots in large bowl. Add red pepper, cucumber, tomato, sunflower kernels and cheese; mix well. Stir in rice. Toss gently with mixture of remaining ingredients. Chill until serving time.
Yield: 3 to 4 servings.

Seafood and Pecan Salad

1¹/₂ pounds shrimp, crab meat or lobster, cooked
3 green onions, finely chopped
1 cup thinly sliced celery
Vanilla Mayonnaise
1 head Boston lettuce, torn
1 cup sliced fresh mushrooms
1 avocado, sliced
1 (8-ounce) can artichoke hearts, drained
¹/₂ cup slivered pecan halves, lightly toasted

*Peel shrimp. Combine shrimp, green onions and celery in bowl. Add enough
Vanilla Mayonnaise to bind the mixture. Add lettuce; toss to mix well. Top with
mushrooms, avocado, artichoke hearts and toasted pecans.*
Yield: 4 to 6 servings.

Vanilla Mayonnaise

1 egg
¹/₂ teaspoon Dijon mustard
¹/₂ teaspoon sugar
1 tablespoon fresh lemon juice
1 tablespoon fruit vinegar
1 cup vegetable oil
1 teaspoon vanilla extract

*Combine egg, mustard, sugar, lemon juice and vinegar in
blender or food processor container; process until smooth. Add a few drops of
oil, processing constantly. Add remaining oil in fine stream, processing
constantly. Stir in vanilla. May whisk in a small amount of additional oil
and vinegar if needed for consistency.*
Yield: 1¹/₂ cups.

Spinach Pecan Salad

1 pound fresh spinach
1 (11-ounce) can mandarin oranges
2 ribs celery, thinly sliced
2 scallions, thinly sliced
1 cup white mushrooms, sliced
$1/3$ cup shredded coconut
$1/2$ cup pecans
Poppy Seed Dressing

*Rinse spinach well; discard stems and tear into bite-size pieces.
Drain mandarin oranges. Combine spinach, celery, scallions, mushrooms
and oranges in a large salad bowl; toss to mix. Sprinkle coconut and
pecans on top. Serve with Poppy Seed Dressing.
Yield: 8 servings.*

Poppy Seed Dressing

$1/2$ cup sugar
1 tablespoon dry mustard
1 teaspoon salt
$1/4$ onion, grated
$1/2$ cup white vinegar
2 cups vegetable oil
$1^{1}/2$ tablespoons poppy seeds

*Blend the sugar, mustard, salt, onion and vinegar in small bowl.
Add oil in a fine stream, whisking constantly. Stir in poppy seeds.
Yield: 3 cups.*

Caesar Croutons

3 tablespoons butter
3 tablespoons olive oil
3 cups ½-inch cubes of dried bread
2 large cloves of garlic, minced
1 teaspoon chopped fresh parsley
1 teaspoon chopped fresh chives
1 teaspoon chopped fresh tarragon
3 tablespoons freshly grated Parmesan cheese

Heat butter and olive oil in large skillet over medium-high heat, stirring until blended. Add bread cubes, tossing to coat well. Reduce heat to medium-low. Add garlic, parsley, chives and tarragon, tossing to coat bread cubes. Cook for 20 minutes or until bread cubes are brown, tossing frequently. Spoon into large bowl; add Parmesan cheese, tossing to coat. Spread on flat surface to cool to room temperature. Store in airtight container.
Yield: 3 cups.

Raspberry Vinaigrette

1 (10-ounce) package frozen unsweetened raspberries, thawed
1 cup vegetable oil
¼ cup raspberry vinegar
2 tablespoons honey
1 clove of garlic

Press raspberries through sieve, discarding seeds. Reserve ³/₄ cup pulp. discarding remaining pulp. Combine reserved raspberry pulp, oil, raspl vinegar, honey and garlic in food processor container. Process until blen.
Yield: 32 servings.

Honey Dijon Salad Dressing

1 cup mayonnaise
1/4 cup Dijon mustard ▪ 1/4 cup honey
3/4 teaspoon cider vinegar ▪ 1/8 teaspoon onion powder
Dash of red pepper ▪ 1/4 cup vegetable oil

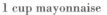

Combine mayonnaise, mustard, honey, vinegar, onion powder and red pepper in blender container. Add oil in a fine stream, processing constantly until smooth. May store, covered, in refrigerator for 2 weeks.
Yield: 1 3/4 cups.

Hot Spinach Dressing

5 ounces bacon ▪ 2 eggs, beaten
3/4 cup sour cream
1/4 cup vinegar ▪ Salt to taste

Fry bacon in skillet until crisp. Drain, reserving 1 tablespoon pan drippings. Crumble bacon. Combine reserved pan drippings, eggs, sour cream, vinegar and salt in saucepan; mix well. Bring to a boil. Remove from heat. Stir in bacon. Serve over fresh or frozen spinach.
Yield: 6 servings.

Lemon Lime Honey Salad Dressing

2 tablespoons lime juice
2 tablespoons lemon juice ▪ 1 tablespoon paprika
1 teaspoon mustard ▪ 1/3 cup honey
3/4 teaspoon salt (optional)
2/3 cup olive oil
1 1/2 tablespoons onion juice

Combine lime juice, lemon juice, paprika, mustard, honey and salt in saucepan. Bring to a boil; reduce heat. Simmer for several minutes. Stir in olive oil and onion juice. Serve over salad of mixed greens, red onion slices and sliced radishes.
Yield: 18 to 20 tablespoons.

Soups • Appetizers • Salads

Entrées

Marinated Chuck Roast

1 (5-ounce) bottle of soy sauce
1/4 cup packed dark brown sugar
1 tablespoon lemon juice ▪ 1/4 cup vinegar
1 tablespoon Worcestershire sauce
1 cup water ▪ 1 chuck roast
Salt and pepper to taste

Combine first 6 ingredients in small bowl; mix well. Place roast in roasting pan. Pour marinade over roast. Marinate, covered, in refrigerator for 6 hours to overnight; drain. Season with salt and pepper. Grill until desired doneness. Yield: variable.

Pulled Brisket Barbecue

1 (4-pound) beef brisket or chuck roast
1 (3 1/2-ounce) bottle of liquid smoke
2 cups chopped onions ▪ 1/4 cup vinegar
1/4 cup packed dark brown sugar
2 tablespoons spicy brown mustard
1/2 lemon, sliced ▪ 1 tablespoon dark molasses
1 cup catsup ▪ 1/2 cup chili sauce
3 tablespoons Worcestershire sauce
1/4 teaspoon hot pepper sauce
1 tablespoon salt ▪ 1/4 teaspoon cayenne
1/4 teaspoon black pepper
10 to 12 whole wheat buns

Place brisket fat side up on rack in roasting pan. Pour liquid smoke over brisket; cover with foil. Roast at 325 degrees for 3 1/2 hours; remove foil. Roast for 30 minutes longer. Remove and cool brisket, reserving pan drippings. Chill brisket and drippings overnight. Remove fat from brisket and surface of drippings, reserving 3 tablespoons of fat from drippings. Pull beef into shreds. Sauté onions in reserved fat in large saucepan over medium heat. Add 1 cup pan drippings and next 12 ingredients; mix well. Simmer for 20 minutes. Add beef. Simmer for 1 hour, adding additional pan drippings if needed for desired consistency. Serve on whole wheat buns. Yield: 10 to 12 servings.

Flank Steak with Stuffing

1 (2-pound) flank steak ▪ 1 large onion, chopped
1 clove of garlic, pressed ▪ 2 tablespoons olive oil
1/2 cup chopped mushrooms ▪ 1/4 cup coarsely chopped pine nuts
1/4 cup chopped parsley
1 1/2 cups soft bread cubes ▪ 1/4 teaspoon oregano
1/4 teaspoon basil ▪ 1/2 teaspoon salt
Freshly ground pepper to taste
1 egg, beaten ▪ 1 tablespoon vegetable oil
1/2 cup white grape juice

Pound steak with meat mallet; score lightly on both sides. Sauté onion and garlic in hot olive oil in skillet until brown. Add mushrooms. Sauté for 2 to 3 minutes. Add pine nuts, parsley, bread cubes, oregano, basil, salt, pepper and egg; mix well and remove from heat. Spread on steak. Roll to enclose filling; secure with string at 2-inch intervals. Brown on all sides in vegetable oil in Dutch oven. Add grape juice. Bake, covered, at 350 degrees for 2 hours. Cut into 1-inch slices; serve with pan juices.
Yield: 6 servings.

Pine nuts turn rancid quickly because of their high fat content. Store in an airtight container in the refrigerator for up to three months, or in the freezer for up to nine months.

Beef Parmigiana

1 (1 1/2-pound) tenderized round steak ▪ 1 egg, beaten
1/3 cup Parmesan cheese ▪ 1/3 cup Italian bread crumbs
1/3 cup corn oil ▪ 1 medium onion, minced
2 cloves of garlic, minced ▪ 1 teaspoon salt
1/4 teaspoon pepper ▪ 1/2 teaspoon sugar
1/2 teaspoon marjoram ▪ 1 (12-ounce) can tomato paste
3 cups hot water ▪ 8 ounces mozzarella cheese, sliced

Cut steak into 2- to 3-inch pieces. Dip in egg; coat with mixture of Parmesan cheese and bread crumbs. Heat oil in skillet. Brown steak on both sides in oil. Arrange in shallow baking dish. Sauté onion and garlic in drippings in same skillet until tender. Stir in seasonings and tomato paste. Stir in hot water gradually. Boil for 5 minutes, stirring to deglaze skillet. Pour 3/4 of the sauce over steak. Top with cheese slices and remaining sauce. Bake at 350 degrees for 1 hour. Serve with spaghetti.
Yield: 4 to 6 servings.

Beef and Chicken Fajitas

1½ pounds chicken breast fillets
1½ pounds skirt steak
1½ cups apple juice
2 tablespoons olive oil
2 teaspoons lime juice
2 teaspoons minced garlic
Worcestershire sauce to taste
½ teaspoon oregano
1 tablespoon coarsely ground pepper
12 flour tortillas
Vegetable Sauté
Sour cream
Shredded Cheddar and Monterey Jack cheeses
Salsa
Shredded lettuce
Sliced black olives

Rinse chicken and pat dry; trim fat from steak. Combine next 7 ingredients in large bowl; mix well. Pour half over chicken and half over beef in separate bowls. Marinate, covered, in refrigerator overnight. Drain, reserving marinades. Grill chicken and steak on covered grill until cooked through, brushing occasionally with marinade. Slice chicken and steak into strips. Sear in hot skillet. Serve with tortillas, Vegetable Sauté and remaining ingredients. Yield: 12 servings.

Vegetable Sauté

1 green bell pepper, sliced
2 or 3 tomatoes, chopped
1 red onion, sliced
Garlic salt and pepper to taste
1 or 2 teaspoons butter or margarine

Sauté green pepper, tomatoes and onion with garlic salt and pepper in butter in large skillet until tender. Keep warm. Yield: 12 servings.

Oven Stew

1$\frac{1}{2}$ to 2 pounds stew beef
4 to 6 potatoes, chopped
4 carrots, thickly sliced
1 onion, sliced
1 head cabbage, cut into large pieces
1 tablespoon sugar
1 cup diagonally sliced celery
3 tablespoons tapioca
1 cup hot water ▪ 1 beef bouillon cube
1 cup tomato juice
1$\frac{1}{2}$ teaspoons salt ▪ 1 slice bread

*Combine beef, potatoes, carrots, onion, cabbage, sugar, celery, tapioca,
hot water, bouillon cube, tomato juice and salt in bowl; mix well.
Spoon into greased baking pan. Crumble bread over top. Bake, covered,
at 325 degrees for 2$\frac{1}{2}$ hours. Serve with French bread.
Yield: 6 to 8 servings.*

Famous Enchilada Casserole

1 pound lean ground beef
$\frac{1}{2}$ cup finely chopped onion
1 teaspoon garlic powder
$\frac{1}{2}$ teaspoon cumin
1 (10-ounce) can mild enchilada sauce
$\frac{1}{2}$ sauce can water
1 (12-count) package corn tortillas
1 cup shredded Cheddar cheese
1 cup shredded Monterey Jack cheese

*Brown ground beef in skillet, stirring until crumbly; drain. Add onion, garlic
powder, cumin, enchilada sauce and water. Simmer over low heat for 15
minutes, stirring occasionally. Layer tortillas, meat sauce, Cheddar cheese and
Monterey Jack cheese $\frac{1}{2}$ at a time in greased casserole. Bake at 325
degrees for 15 minutes or until brown and bubbly. May add a few drops of
Tabasco sauce to meat sauce to make more spicy.
Yield: 6 servings.*

*Buy nuts in quantity
and store them
in airtight containers
in the freezer.
Freezing retains the
freshness and flavor.*

Ground Beef and Noodle Bake

2 pounds (or more) ground beef
2 tablespoons butter
2 (8-ounce) cans tomato sauce
1 teaspoon sugar
1 teaspoon salt
Pepper to taste
1 (8-ounce) package noodles, cooked, drained
8 ounces cream cheese, chopped
1 cup sour cream
3 green onions, chopped
1/2 cup shredded mild Cheddar cheese

*Brown ground beef in butter in skillet, stirring until crumbly; drain. Add
tomato sauce, sugar, salt and pepper; mix well. Simmer, covered, for 15
minutes. Layer noodles, cream cheese, sour cream, green onions and ground
beef mixture 1/2 at a time in greased large baking dish. Top with cheese. Bake
at 350 degrees for 30 to 45 minutes or until heated through.
Yield: 8 servings.*

Spaghetti Pizza

1 pound ground beef
12 ounces spaghetti
2 eggs
1/2 cup milk
1 cup shredded mozzarella cheese
1 (32-ounce) jar spaghetti sauce
3 cups shredded mozzarella cheese

*Brown ground beef in skillet, stirring until crumbly; drain. Break spaghetti
into 2-inch pieces. Cook using package directions; rinse and drain. Combine
with eggs, milk and 1 cup mozzarella cheese in bowl; mix well. Spread in
greased 10x15-inch baking pan. Bake at 400 degrees for 15 minutes. Spread
with spaghetti sauce. Crumble ground beef over top; sprinkle with 3 cups
mozzarella cheese. Bake at 350 degrees for 30 minutes. May add olives,
mushrooms, onions and green peppers or other favorite pizza toppings.
Yield: 16 servings.*

Entrées

White Lasagna

1 pound ground beef
3 tablespoons margarine
1/2 cup chopped onion
1 clove of garlic, minced
1 pound mushrooms
1/3 cup parsley flakes
1/4 cup melted margarine
6 tablespoons flour
2 cups half-and-half
2 cups milk
1/2 cup white grape juice
1 teaspoon salt
1/2 teaspoon pepper
1/4 teaspoon nutmeg
2 eggs, lightly beaten
3 cups ricotta cheese
1 cup shredded mozzarella cheese
4 ounces bleu cheese, crumbled
1/2 cup Parmesan cheese
1 (8-ounce) package lasagna noodles
Paprika

Brown ground beef in 3 tablespoons margarine in skillet, stirring until crumbly. Add onion and garlic. Sauté for 5 minutes. Add mushrooms and parsley. Cook for 5 minutes. Set aside. Blend 1/4 cup melted margarine and flour in saucepan. Cook for 5 minutes, stirring constantly. Stir in half-and-half, milk and grape juice. Cook until thickened, stirring constantly. Stir in seasonings and ground beef mixture. Combine eggs, ricotta cheese, mozzarella cheese and bleu cheese in bowl. Add half the Parmesan cheese; mix well. Spoon a small amount of sauce into 9x13-inch baking pan. Layer noodles, cheese mixture and sauce 1/2 at a time in prepared pan. Sprinkle with remaining Parmesan cheese and paprika. Bake at 375 degrees for 35 to 40 minutes. Let stand for 10 minutes before cutting.
Yield: 8 servings.

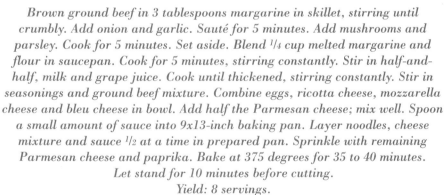

Pork Chop Apple Bake

6 large (1-inch) pork chops
2 tablespoons butter
2 tablespoons steak sauce
6 cups sliced firm cooking apples
$^{1}/_{2}$ teaspoon grated lemon peel
1$^{1}/_{2}$ tablespoons lemon juice
$^{1}/_{4}$ teaspoon nutmeg ▪ $^{1}/_{2}$ teaspoon cinnamon
$^{3}/_{4}$ cup packed brown sugar
2 tablespoons butter ▪ $^{1}/_{4}$ cup hot water

*Brown the pork chops in 2 tablespoons butter in a heavy skillet.
Arrange the chops in a baking dish and sprinkle with the steak sauce. Mix
the apples, lemon peel, lemon juice, nutmeg, cinnamon and brown
sugar in a bowl. Spoon over the chops and dot with 2 tablespoons butter.
Add the hot water. Bake, covered, at 350 degrees for 30 minutes. Bake,
uncovered, for 30 minutes longer or until cooked through.
Yield: 6 servings.*

Peachy Pork Chops and Stuffing

1 (8-ounce) can sliced peaches
$^{1}/_{4}$ cup packed light brown sugar
$^{1}/_{4}$ cup catsup ▪ 2 tablespoons vinegar
6 ($^{3}/_{4}$-inch) thick pork chops
Salt and pepper to taste ▪ 1 tablespoon corn oil
1 package stove-top stuffing mix for pork
1$^{1}/_{2}$ cups very hot water

*Drain peaches, reserving $^{1}/_{3}$ cup syrup. Combine reserved syrup with
brown sugar, catsup and vinegar in saucepan. Simmer for several minutes.
Sprinkle pork chops with salt and pepper. Brown on both sides in oil
in large skillet; remove to 9x13-inch baking dish. Brush with glaze. Bake at 350
degrees for 35 minutes. Prepare stuffing mix with water in same skillet using
package directions. Move pork chops to end of baking dish. Spoon stuffing
into baking dish. Arrange peaches around chops; brush with remaining
glaze. Bake for 20 minutes longer.
Yield: 6 servings.*

Crustless Quiche

2 cups chopped green onions
4 ounces fresh mushrooms, sliced
4 ounces cooked ham, cut into thin strips
3 tablespoons butter
2½ cups whipping cream
6 eggs, beaten
½ teaspoon nutmeg
½ teaspoon salt
Pepper to taste
1½ cups shredded Swiss cheese

Sauté green onions, mushrooms and ham in butter in skillet. Spoon into buttered 7x11-inch baking dish. Combine cream, eggs, seasonings and cheese in bowl; mix well. Pour over ham mixture. Bake at 375 degrees for 30 minutes or until set. Let stand for 10 minutes to cool slightly.
Yield: 8 servings.

Chicken and Dumplings

1 (2½-pound) chicken
1 (8-count) package flour tortillas
½ cup butter
Salt and pepper to taste
2 tablespoons flour
½ cup milk

Rinse chicken and pat dry. Cook in water to cover in large saucepan until tender. Remove chicken, reserving broth; bone chicken. Cut tortillas into bite-sized pieces. Drop into boiling broth in saucepan. Add butter, salt and pepper. Cook until tortillas are very tender. Add chicken. Blend flour and milk in small bowl or covered jar. Stir into saucepan. Cook until thickened, stirring constantly.
Yield: 6 servings.

Oven-Barbecued Chicken

1 (3-pound) chicken, cut up, skinned
1/2 cup flour ▪ 1/3 cup chopped onion
3 tablespoons butter ▪ 1 cup catsup
1/3 cup vinegar ▪ 2 tablespoons brown sugar
1/2 cup water ▪ 2 teaspoons prepared mustard
1 tablespoon Worcestershire sauce
Salt to taste ▪ 1/8 teaspoon pepper

Rinse chicken and pat dry; coat with flour. Brown on all sides in nonstick skillet. Arrange chicken in 9x13-inch baking pan. Bring onion, butter, catsup, vinegar, brown sugar, water, prepared mustard, Worcestershire sauce, salt and pepper to a boil in saucepan, stirring occasionally. Pour over chicken. Bake, covered, at 325 degrees for 1 hour; remove cover. Bake for 15 minutes longer. Yield: 8 servings.

Chicken Breasts with Spinach Dressing

4 whole boned chicken breasts, skinned
1 teaspoon salt
1 (10-ounce) package chopped spinach, thawed
4 ounces mushrooms, chopped
1 cup chopped celery ▪ 1/2 cup chopped onion
1/4 cup melted butter or margarine
3 cups fresh bread crumbs ▪ 1 cup ricotta cheese
1 egg ▪ 1/2 cup melted butter or margarine
1 tablespoon minced parsley
1/2 teaspoon poultry seasoning
1/8 teaspoon pepper ▪ Melted butter or margarine

Cut chicken breasts into halves; rinse and pat dry. Pound 1/4 inch thick; sprinkle with salt. Press spinach to remove moisture. Sauté mushrooms, celery and onion in 1/4 cup butter in medium skillet over medium heat until tender; remove from heat. Stir in spinach and next 7 ingredients; mix well. Spoon onto chicken fillets. Roll chicken to enclose filling; secure with wooden picks. Arrange on rack in 10x14-inch baking pan; brush with additional butter. Bake at 325 degrees for 45 to 60 minutes. May slice to serve if desired. Yield: 8 servings.

Entrées

Raspberry Chicken

8 boneless skinless chicken breast halves
5 ounces low-sugar raspberry preserves
$1/2$ cup thawed pineapple juice concentrate
$1/4$ cup low-sodium soy sauce
2 tablespoons rice vinegar ▪ $1/2$ teaspoon chili powder
$1/2$ teaspoon freshly pressed garlic
$1/2$ cup chopped fresh basil ▪ $1/2$ cup fresh raspberries

Rinse chicken and pat dry; place in rectangular baking dish. Combine preserves, pineapple juice, soy sauce, vinegar, chili powder, garlic and basil in bowl; mix well. Pour over chicken. Marinate, covered, in refrigerator for several hours to overnight. Bake in sauce at 350 degrees for 30 minutes. Place chicken on serving platter. Top with sauce and raspberries. Freezes well.
Yield: 8 servings.

Crush nuts quickly and easily with a rolling pin.

Walnut - Stuffed Chicken Breasts

6 chicken breasts, cut into halves
1 cup shredded Cheddar cheese
$1/2$ cup chopped walnuts ▪ $1/2$ cup fresh bread crumbs
2 tablespoons minced onion ▪ $1/2$ teaspoon salt
$1/8$ teaspoon pepper ▪ $1/2$ cup flour ▪ 3 tablespoons butter
$1^1/2$ cups chicken stock
2 tablespoons chopped parsley ▪ Parsley sprigs

Rinse chicken and pat dry. Bone and skin chicken breast halves. Pound each to $1/4$-inch thickness between 2 sheets of waxed paper. Combine cheese, walnuts, bread crumbs, onion, salt and pepper in bowl; mix well. Spoon $1^1/2$ tablespoons of cheese mixture onto each chicken breast half, spreading mixture to within $1/2$ inch of edges. Roll as for jelly roll from narrow end. Secure with wooden pick. Dredge with flour. Let stand for 10 minutes. Sauté in butter in large skillet until light brown. Pour chicken stock over chicken. Simmer, covered, over low heat for 20 minutes. Remove chicken to warm platter, reserving cooking liquid. Remove wooden picks. Cook liquid over high heat until slightly thickened, stirring frequently. Stir in 2 tablespoons chopped parsley. Pour sauce over chicken. Top with parsley sprigs.
Yield: 6 servings.

Entrées

Cashew Chicken

Cashews have a sweet buttery flavor. The flavor is enchanced if the nuts are lightly toasted.

12 ounces boneless skinless chicken, cut into strips
3 cloves of garlic ▪ 1 tablespoon ground ginger
1 tablespoon soy sauce
1½ tablespoons vegetable oil ▪ 3 cups broccoli florets
1 cup snow pea pods, cut into halves
1½ cups water
⅓ cup dry chicken noodle soup mix
2 tablespoons cornstarch ▪ 1 cup sliced radishes
½ cup lightly salted cashews
4 cups cooked rice

Rinse chicken and pat dry. Combine garlic, ginger and soy sauce in bowl; mix well. Add chicken; coat well. Heat oil in wok. Stir-fry broccoli for 1 minute. Add snow peas. Cook for 3 minutes or until tender-crisp. Remove to plate. Add chicken to wok; brown. Add water, soup mix and cornstarch. Simmer, covered, for 5 minutes. Return sautéed vegetables to wok. Add radishes and cashews. Cook until hot. Serve over cooked rice.
Yield: 4 to 6 servings.

Chicken Dijon Fettuccini

2 pounds boneless skinless chicken breasts
1½ teaspoons salt ▪ ¼ teaspoon pepper
¼ cup margarine ▪ 2 cups whipping cream
⅓ cup Dijon mustard ▪ ¼ cup chopped fresh parsley
2 tablespoons minced fresh chives
9 ounces uncooked fettuccini

Rinse chicken and pat dry. Cut into 1-inch pieces. Sprinkle with salt and pepper. Sauté chicken in margarine in large heavy skillet for 4 to 7 minutes or until no longer pink and cooked through. Remove chicken from skillet. Stir cream and mustard into pan drippings. Bring to a boil, stirring constantly; reduce heat. Simmer for 8 minutes or until slightly thickened. Return chicken to skillet. Add parsley and chives. Heat to serving temperature; do not boil. Cook fettuccini using package directions; drain well. Toss chicken mixture with hot fettuccini. Serve immediately.
Yield: 6 servings.

Chicken Linguini Stir-Fry

1 pound chicken breast strips ▪ 1 (16-ounce) package fresh linguini
Olive oil ▪ 2 cloves of garlic, finely minced
Ginger to taste ▪ 2 carrots, peeled, thinly sliced
2 cups broccoli florets ▪ 2 cups cauliflowerets
1 small red bell pepper, julienned
4 cups fresh spinach ▪ ¹/₂ cup chopped green onions
1 cup red wine vinegar ▪ ¹/₄ cup soy sauce

*Rinse chicken and pat dry. Cook linguini according to package directions;
drain. Heat 2 tablespoons olive oil in large skillet or wok over medium-high
heat. Add garlic and ginger. Sauté for 1 minute. Add chicken. Sauté for 5
minutes. Add carrots, broccoli, cauliflower and red pepper. Sauté for 5
minutes. Add 1 tablespoon oil at a time as necessary. Add spinach and green
onions. Sauté for 2 minutes. Transfer to large bowl. Add linguini; mix well. Mix
vinegar, soy sauce and 2 to 4 tablespoons olive oil in same skillet. Simmer
for 1 minute. Toss sauce and linguini mixture together.
Yield: 8 servings.*

Chicken Stew with Dumplings

2 to 2¹/₂ pounds chicken breasts ▪ 5 cups water
4 potatoes, chopped ▪ 3 carrots, cut into quarters
2 ribs celery, sliced ▪ 1 medium onion, cut into eighths
1 (10-ounce) package frozen peas ▪ Salt and pepper to taste
1¹/₂ cups flour ▪ 2 teaspoons baking powder ▪ ³/₄ teaspoon salt
3 tablespoons butter or margarine, softened
1 cup milk ▪ ¹/₂ cup chopped parsley

*Rinse chicken; combine with water in heavy saucepan. Cook, covered, over
medium heat for 50 minutes or until tender. Remove and chop chicken,
discarding skin and bones. Return chicken to broth. Add next 5 ingredients.
Simmer, covered, over medium heat for 15 minutes or until vegetables are
tender. Season with salt and pepper. Mix flour, baking powder and ³/₄ teaspoon
salt in bowl. Cut in butter until crumbly. Stir in milk and parsley. Drop by
rounded tablespoonfuls into hot stew. Cook, uncovered, for 10 minutes. Cook,
covered, for 8 minutes longer or until dumplings are cooked through.
Yield: 8 servings.*

Water chestnuts are available canned in most supermarkets, and fresh in most Oriental markets. The fresh are the best in quality.

Chinese - Style Chicken

2 chicken breasts, skinned, cooked
1 medium yellow onion ▪ 3 ribs celery
4 green onions with stems
1 (4-ounce) can bamboo shoots
6 water chestnuts ▪ 2 ounces fresh mushrooms
1¹/₂ cups fresh bean sprouts ▪ 2 tablespoons vegetable oil
3 tablespoons lemon juice ▪ 2 tablespoons sesame seeds

Chop chicken into ¹/₄-inch pieces. Slice onion, celery, green onions, bamboo shoots, chestnuts and mushrooms into thin strips. Stir-fry sliced vegetables and bean sprouts in oil in wok or skillet for 3 minutes; remove to serving bowl. Add chicken, lemon juice and sesame seeds to wok. Stir-fry for 1 minute. Add to vegetables; mix lightly. Serve over brown rice.
Yield: 4 servings.

Lemonade Chicken

4 boneless skinless chicken breasts
1 medium green bell pepper ▪ 1 medium red bell pepper
1 medium yellow bell pepper or 1 small summer squash
1 cup white rice ▪ 2 tablespoons vegetable oil
2 cloves of garlic, minced
1 (6-ounce) can frozen lemonade concentrate
¹/₄ cup water
1 tablespoon instant chicken bouillon
¹/₄ cup water ▪ 2 teaspoons cornstarch

Rinse chicken and pat dry. Cut chicken into ¹/₂x2-inch strips. Cut peppers into 1-inch strips. Cook rice using package directions; keep warm. Heat oil in 10-inch skillet over medium-high heat. Add chicken and garlic. Stir-fry until chicken is opaque. Reduce heat to medium. Add lemonade concentrate, ¹/₄ cup water and bouillon; mix well. Cook for 10 minutes or until liquid is reduced by half. Add pepper strips. Cook, covered, for 5 minutes or until peppers are tender-crisp. Blend ¹/₄ cup water with cornstarch. Pour into skillet. Bring mixture to a boil, stirring constantly. Cook for 1 minute. Serve chicken and peppers over rice.
Yield: 4 servings.

Chicken Lasagna

1 green bell pepper, chopped
$^1/_2$ onion, chopped
1 (6-ounce) can mushrooms, drained
1 (10-ounce) can cream of chicken soup
1 (4-ounce) jar pimentos, drained
$^1/_2$ teaspoon basil
6 lasagna noodles, cooked
3 cups chopped cooked chicken
2 cups (or more) shredded Cheddar cheese
1$^1/_2$ cups cottage cheese
Parmesan cheese

Sauté green pepper and onion in large nonstick skillet until tender. Remove from heat. Add mushrooms, soup, pimentos and basil; mix well. Layer noodles, chicken, Cheddar cheese, cottage cheese and sauce $^1/_2$ at a time in greased 7x11-inch baking dish. Sprinkle with Parmesan cheese. Bake at 350 degrees for 45 to 60 minutes or until brown and bubbly. Let stand at room temperature for 10 minutes before serving.
Yield: 6 servings.

Chicken Potpie

2 cups chopped cooked chicken
2 (10-ounce) cans cream of potato soup
$^1/_2$ cup milk
1 (16-ounce) can mixed vegetables, drained
1 package all-ready refrigerator pie pastry

Combine chicken, soup, milk and vegetables in bowl; mix gently. Spoon into pastry-lined 9-inch deep-dish pie plate. Top with remaining pastry. Flute and trim edge; cut vents. Bake at 375 degrees for 40 minutes or until brown.
Yield: 6 servings.

Mexican Baked Flounder

¹/₄ cup chopped onion
2 cloves of garlic, minced
1 tablespoon vegetable oil
1 (16-ounce) can tomatoes, drained, chopped
1 tablespoon chopped green chiles
1 teaspoon chili powder ▪ ¹/₈ teaspoon pepper
1 egg white ▪ 1 tablespoon skim milk
4 (4-ounce) flounder fillets ▪ ¹/₂ cup cornmeal
¹/₂ cup shredded part-skim mozzarella cheese

Sauté onion and garlic in oil in medium saucepan over medium heat for 3 minutes or until soft. Add tomatoes, chiles, chili powder and pepper. Simmer, covered, for 15 minutes, stirring occasionally. Beat egg white and skim milk in shallow dish. Dip fillets in egg mixture and coat with cornmeal. Place in single layer in baking dish sprayed with nonstick cooking spray. Spoon sauce over fillets and sprinkle with cheese. Bake at 350 degrees for 20 minutes or until fish flakes easily. Garnish with avocado slices and dollop of fat-free sour cream.
Yield: 4 servings.

Fillets of Flounder

10 ounces frozen chopped spinach
1 cup cooked brown rice
¹/₄ cup thinly sliced green onions
¹/₄ cup toasted chopped almonds
¹/₄ teaspoon salt ▪ ¹/₄ teaspoon pepper
¹/₄ teaspoon nutmeg ▪ 6 fillets of flounder
1 (10-ounce) can cream of mushroom soup
¹/₄ cup light cream ▪ Paprika

Combine first 7 ingredients in small bowl. Arrange fish fillets in single layer on 18x26-inch piece of heavy-duty cooking foil. Spread ¹/₄ cup spinach mixture on each fillet. Fold to enclose filling; secure with wooden pick. Combine soup and cream in medium bowl; mix well. Pour over fish; seal foil. Bake at 350 degrees for 1 hour or until fish flakes. Sprinkle with paprika.
Yield: 6 servings.

Stuffed Orange Roughy

1/2 cup finely chopped onion
1 teaspoon olive oil ▪ 1/4 cup brown rice
1/4 cup wild rice ▪ 1 cup chicken broth
1/4 teaspoon mustard seeds ▪ 1/4 teaspoon dried thyme leaves
1/4 teaspoon rubbed sage ▪ 1 cup sliced small mushrooms
1 1/4 pounds fresh orange roughy, cut into 4 equal fillets
1/4 cup bread crumbs ▪ 1 small clove of garlic, minced
2 tablespoons minced fresh parsley
1 tablespoon minced scallions ▪ 1 tablespoon olive oil

Sauté onion in 1 teaspoon oil in saucepan for 2 minutes. Add next 6 ingredients. Bring to a boil; reduce heat. Simmer, covered, for 40 to 50 minutes. Add mushrooms. Simmer for 5 minutes longer. Coat large shallow casserole with nonstick cooking spray. Place 4 mounds of mushroom mixture in casserole. Arrange 1 fillet over each mound. Mix remaining ingredients in bowl. Spoon over fillets. Bake at 400 degrees for 10 minutes or until golden brown. Yield: 4 servings.

Cheesy Picante Orange Roughy

2 chicken bouillon cubes ▪ 3 tablespoons hot water
1 small can mushrooms, drained
1 medium green bell pepper, cut into 1-inch pieces
1 medium onion, chopped ▪ 1 cup sliced carrots
6 (4-ounce) fillets orange roughy
Seasoned salt to taste ▪ 2 tablespoons Parmesan cheese
1/2 cup each shredded Cheddar cheese and baby Swiss cheese
1/4 cup shredded mozzarella cheese
2 cups mild picante sauce

Dissolve bouillon in hot water in microwave-safe casserole. Add mushrooms, green pepper, onion and carrots; mix well. Microwave on High for 8 to 10 minutes or until tender-crisp. Arrange fish in single layer in 8-inch-square glass baking dish. Sprinkle with seasoned salt. Microwave on High for 4 to 5 minutes or until fish flakes easily; drain. Spoon vegetables over fish. Sprinkle with cheeses; add picante sauce. Microwave for 8 minutes or until cheeses melt. Yield: 4 to 6 servings.

Ocean Perch Supreme

2 tablespoons butter or margarine, softened
1¹/₂ pounds frozen ocean perch
2 tablespoons fresh lemon juice ▪ ¹/₂ cup milk
1 (10-ounce) can cream of mushroom soup
¹/₂ cup water ▪ 1 teaspoon tarragon
2 tablespoons toasted sliced almonds

*Spread half the butter in 9x13-inch baking dish. Arrange fish in dish.
Spread with remaining butter; sprinkle with lemon juice. Combine milk, soup,
water and tarragon in bowl; mix well. Spoon over fish. Bake at 400 degrees
for 30 minutes. Sprinkle with almonds.
Yield: 4 servings.*

Grilled Barbecued Salmon

2¹/₂ pounds fresh salmon fillets ▪ Salt and pepper to taste
Lemon juice to taste ▪ Barbecue Sauce for Fish

*Rinse salmon and pat dry. Sprinkle with salt, pepper and lemon
juice. Baste fillets with Barbecue Sauce for Fish. Place on 2 layers of heavy-
duty foil. Place foil over medium coals. Grill just until salmon begins
to flake, basting frequently. Baste again just before serving. Serve with
fresh peas and new potatoes.
Yield: 6 servings.*

Barbecue Sauce for Fish

1 cup butter
2 or more cloves of garlic, minced
¹/₄ cup soy sauce
2 tablespoons Dijon mustard
Dash of Worcestershire sauce
Dash of catsup

*Combine butter, garlic, soy sauce, mustard, Worcestershire sauce and catsup in
small saucepan. Heat until well blended, stirring frequently; do not boil.
Yield: 1¹/₄ cups.*

Salmon Corn Cakes

3 eggs ▪ 2 tablespoons flour
2 teaspoons lemon juice
2 drops of red pepper sauce
1 teaspoon salt ▪ Pepper to taste
1 (12-ounce) can whole kernel corn, drained
1 (7-ounce) can salmon, drained, flaked
1/2 cup sour cream
1/4 cup shredded American cheese
2 tablespoons chopped pimento

*Combine eggs, flour, lemon juice, pepper sauce, salt and pepper in bowl;
beat with rotary beater until foamy. Stir in corn and salmon. Drop by generous
1/4 cupfuls onto hot greased griddle; press lightly to flatten. Bake for 3 minutes
on each side or until golden brown. Combine sour cream, cheese and pimento
in saucepan. Cook over low heat just until bubbly, stirring constantly.
Serve with salmon corn cakes.
Yield: 4 servings.*

Fish Roll-Ups Florentine

1 (10-ounce) package frozen chopped spinach
3 eggs, beaten ▪ 1 1/2 cups herb-seasoned stuffing mix
1/2 cup shredded Cheddar cheese
1 pound sole fillets
1 (10-ounce) can cream of mushroom soup
1/2 cup sour cream ▪ 2 tablespoons lemon juice

*Microwave spinach in package on Defrost for 4 to 6 minutes. Let stand for 5
minutes or until thawed; drain well. Combine with eggs, stuffing mix and
cheese in bowl; mix well. Spoon onto fish fillets. Roll to enclose filling; secure
with wooden picks. Place seam side down in 7x11-inch baking dish. Combine
soup, sour cream and lemon juice in bowl; mix well. Spoon half the
soup mixture over fish. Microwave, covered with plastic wrap, on High for 10
to 12 minutes or until fish flakes easily, rotating dish 1/2 turn after 5 minutes.
Microwave remaining sauce, covered, on High for 1 1/2 to 2 1/2 minutes
or until heated through. Spoon over fish to serve.
Yield: 4 servings.*

Clam Fritters

2 (8-ounce) cans minced clams, drained
2 egg yolks, beaten
1 cup dry bread crumbs
2 teaspoons each chopped parsley and chives
1 teaspoon salt
$1/2$ teaspoon pepper
$1/2$ cup milk
2 egg whites
Vegetable oil for frying

Combine clams, egg yolks, bread crumbs, parsley, chives, salt, pepper and milk in bowl; mix well. Beat egg whites until stiff peaks form. Fold gently into batter. Drop by tablespoonfuls into $1/2$ inch hot oil in skillet. Fry until golden brown, turning once; drain on paper towels. Arrange on serving plate. Garnish with orange slices.
Yield: 6 servings.

Linguini with Clam Sauce

1 (10-ounce) can clams
2 tablespoons minced onion
2 tablespoons minced celery
3 tablespoons margarine
$3/4$ cup sliced mushrooms
2 tablespoons flour
1 cup milk
1 tablespoon chopped parsley
Salt and pepper to taste
1 (16-ounce) package linguini, cooked

Drain clams, reserving liquid; chop clams. Sauté onion and celery in margarine in small saucepan. Add mushrooms. Cook for 2 to 3 minutes or until tender. Stir in flour. Add reserved clam liquid and milk. Cook until thickened, stirring constantly. Add clams, parsley, salt and pepper. Cook until heated through. Serve over linguini. Serve with tossed salad and dinner rolls.
Yield: 8 servings.

Entrées

Scallops with Spinach Fettuccini

8 ounces spinach fettuccini
1 tablespoon butter
1 tablespoon vegetable oil
1 medium onion, chopped
1 carrot, finely chopped
1 pound bay scallops
1/4 cup white grape juice
1 (16-ounce) can tomatoes
1 teaspoon dill
1/2 to 1 teaspoon oregano
1 clove of garlic, minced
Salt and pepper to taste
Shredded fresh Parmesan cheese

Frozen nuts

are easier to chop.

Cook fettuccini using package directions; drain. Melt butter with oil in large skillet. Add onion, carrot and scallops; toss to mix. Cook over medium heat for several minutes, stirring constantly. Add grape juice, tomatoes, dill, oregano and garlic; mix well. Cook over medium heat until liquid is absorbed. Stir in salt and pepper. Add fettuccini; toss to mix. Sprinkle with Parmesan cheese.
Yield: 4 servings.

Marinated Shrimp

1 pound shrimp, cooked, peeled
2 medium purple onions, sliced into rings
2 to 3 bay leaves ▪ 1 cup vegetable oil
1/4 cup cider vinegar ▪ 1/4 cup catsup
2 tablespoons Worcestershire sauce
2 teaspoons sugar
1/4 teaspoon dry mustard
1 teaspoon salt
Red pepper to taste

Layer shrimp, onions and bay leaves in bowl. Combine oil, vinegar, catsup, Worcestershire sauce, sugar, dry mustard, salt and red pepper in small bowl; mix well. Pour over layers. Marinate in refrigerator for up to 2 days.
Yield: 2 servings.

Cream Cheese Mushroom Enchiladas

1/2 cup chopped onion
1 clove of garlic, minced
1 tablespoon vegetable oil
1 (28-ounce) can Italian seasoned tomatoes, cut up
1 tablespoon honey
1 tablespoon chili powder
1/2 teaspoon ground cumin
1/2 teaspoon ground coriander
Ground red pepper to taste
12 ounces fresh mushrooms, sliced
1 1/2 teaspoons chili powder
2 tablespoons margarine
8 ounces cream cheese
1 cup sour cream
3/4 cup thinly sliced green onions
8 (7-inch) flour tortillas
3/4 cup shredded Monterey Jack cheese

Sauté onion and garlic in oil in skillet until tender. Stir in undrained tomatoes, honey, 1 tablespoon chili powder, cumin, coriander and pepper. Bring to a boil; reduce heat. Simmer for 30 minutes or until thickened, stirring occasionally. Cook mushrooms with 1 1/2 teaspoons chili powder and margarine in saucepan over medium-high heat for 4 minutes or until liquid has evaporated; reduce heat. Add cream cheese, stirring until melted. Stir in sour cream and green onions. Spoon 1/3 cup cream cheese mixture into center of each tortilla; roll up. Place seam side down in 7x12-inch baking dish. Spoon tomato mixture over enchiladas. Sprinkle with Monterey Jack cheese. Bake, covered, at 350 degrees for 30 minutes.
Yield: 8 servings.

Eggplant - Stuffed Shells

8 ounces jumbo macaroni shells or tubes
1 large clove of garlic, thinly sliced
1/4 cup vegetable oil
1 (1-pound) eggplant, peeled, chopped
1/2 cup finely chopped onion
1/2 cup water
1 (32-ounce) jar spaghetti sauce
1 cup low-fat cottage cheese
4 egg whites
1/2 cup Italian-style bread crumbs
1 teaspoon oregano
1/8 teaspoon pepper
8 ounces mozzarella cheese, sliced

Cook macaroni shells al dente using package directions; rinse with water and drain. Sauté garlic in oil in skillet until brown; discard garlic. Add eggplant and onion to garlic oil. Sauté for 5 minutes. Add water. Simmer, covered, for 10 minutes or until tender, stirring occasionally. Cool. Pour half the spaghetti sauce into 9x13-inch baking pan. Combine cottage cheese, egg whites, bread crumbs, oregano and pepper in bowl; mix well. Add eggplant mixture; mix well. Spoon into macaroni shells; arrange in prepared baking pan. Pour remaining spaghetti sauce over shells. Top with mozzarella cheese. Bake, covered, at 375 degrees for 20 minutes. Bake, uncovered, for 10 minutes longer. May be prepared and refrigerated until ready to bake. Add an additional 10 minutes to covered baking time if chilled.
Yield: 8 servings.

Italian Manicotti

16 uncooked manicotti shells
2 cups low-fat cottage cheese
1 cup grated Parmesan cheese
1 cup shredded low-fat mozzarella cheese
2 eggs, slightly beaten
1 teaspoon oregano
1/4 cup fresh chopped parsley
1/4 teaspoon cayenne pepper
2 (16-ounce) cans stewed tomatoes
1 1/2 tablespoons Italian seasoning
2 tablespoons cornstarch

Cook manicotti using package directions. Drain; place in cold water. Combine cottage cheese, Parmesan cheese, mozzarella cheese, eggs, oregano, parsley and cayenne pepper in bowl; mix well. Drain manicotti. Stuff shells with cheese mixture. Arrange in lightly oiled 9x13-inch baking pan. Combine stewed tomatoes, Italian seasoning and cornstarch in saucepan; mix well. Bring to a boil. Cook until thickened, stirring constantly. Pour over stuffed manicotti. Bake, covered, at 350 degrees for 40 to 50 minutes.
Yield: 8 servings.

Meatless Sauce and Pasta Dinner

1 (9-ounce) can tomatoes
1 (10-ounce) can Ro-Tel tomatoes
1 clove of garlic, chopped
1 tablespoon Worcestershire sauce
1 tablespoon basil ▪ 1 teaspoon oregano
1 tablespoon wine vinegar
1 (16-ounce) jar mushroom pieces or 1 can white beans
Salt and pepper to taste ▪ 1 onion, sliced
4 cups cooked pasta

Combine first 10 ingredients in large skillet; mix well. Place onion slices on top. Cook over medium-high heat for 15 minutes. Reduce heat; simmer, covered, for 1 hour. Serve over pasta.
Yield: 4 servings.

Entrées

Spinach Lasagna

1 (10-ounce) package frozen chopped spinach
1 pound lasagna noodles
8 ounces mozzarella cheese, shredded
4 ounces egg substitute
Easy Tomato Sauce
2^1/2 cups low-fat cottage cheese
^{1}/2 cup Parmesan cheese

Cook spinach using package directions; drain and rinse in cold water. Cook lasagna noodles using package directions; drain. Combine spinach, mozzarella cheese and egg substitute in bowl; mix well. Coat baking dish with nonstick cooking spray. Layer ^{1}/3 of the Easy Tomato Sauce, ^{1}/2 of the noodles and ^{1}/2 of the spinach mixture in prepared baking dish. Top with half the remaining sauce, half the cottage cheese and remaining noodles. Layer remaining spinach mixture, cottage cheese and sauce on top. Sprinkle with Parmesan cheese. Bake at 350 degrees for 40 minutes. Let stand for 10 minutes before serving. Yield: 10 servings.

Easy Tomato Sauce

1 large onion, chopped
1 green bell pepper, chopped
3 tablespoons olive oil
1 (32-ounce) jar spaghetti sauce
1 tablespoon oregano
1 (6-ounce) can salt-free tomato paste
1 bay leaf
^{1}/2 teaspoon salt
^{1}/4 cup parsley flakes

Sauté onion and green pepper in olive oil in heavy skillet for 5 minutes. Add spaghetti sauce, oregano, tomato paste, bay leaf, salt and parsley flakes; stir well. Simmer for 30 minutes; remove bay leaf. Yield: 10 servings.

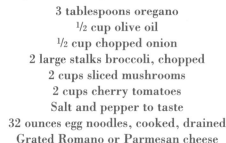

Pasta Primavera

3 tablespoons oregano
¹/₂ cup olive oil
¹/₂ cup chopped onion
2 large stalks broccoli, chopped
2 cups sliced mushrooms
2 cups cherry tomatoes
Salt and pepper to taste
32 ounces egg noodles, cooked, drained
Grated Romano or Parmesan cheese

Sauté oregano in hot olive oil in 16-inch skillet for 1 minute. Add onion. Sauté for 2 minutes. Increase heat to medium-high. Add broccoli, mushrooms and tomatoes. Cook for 12 minutes. Season with salt and pepper. Toss with hot pasta in serving bowl. Serve with cheese. May serve chilled if desired.
Yield: 4 to 6 servings.

Vegetable-Stuffed Shells

¹/₂ cup chopped leeks, white part only
2 teaspoons margarine
¹/₂ cup coarsely shredded carrot
¹/₂ cup coarsely shredded yellow squash
¹/₂ cup coarsely shredded zucchini
¹/₄ teaspoon dried basil
1¹/₂ ounces jumbo pasta shells, cooked, drained
1 ounce coarsely shredded Monterey Jack cheese

Sauté leeks in margarine in large nonstick skillet over medium-high heat for 5 minutes or until tender. Add carrot, squash and zucchini; mix well. Cook for 3 minutes or until vegetables are tender. Stir in basil. Fill shells with vegetable mixture; sprinkle with cheese. Place in 8-inch-square baking pan sprayed with nonstick cooking spray. Bake, covered, at 350 degrees for 15 minutes.
Yield: 2 servings.

Side Dishes Breads

Marinated Asparagus

2 pounds fresh asparagus ▪ ⅓ cup chopped parsley
⅓ cup sliced black olives ▪ ⅓ cup sliced green olives
2 ounces pimento ▪ 2 tablespoons chopped green onions
1½ cups vegetable oil ▪ ½ cup red wine vinegar
2 teaspoons lemon juice ▪ 1 teaspoon Worcestershire sauce
1 tablespoon dried basil ▪ 2 teaspoons ground pepper
1 teaspoon dried oregano ▪ ½ teaspoon garlic powder
½ teaspoon salt ▪ ¼ teaspoon sugar

*Cook asparagus in a small amount of water in covered saucepan for 6 to
8 minutes or until tender; drain. Place in 9x13-inch shallow dish.
Arrange parsley, olives, pimento and green onions over asparagus. Combine
remaining ingredients in container; cover and shake well. Pour over
asparagus. Chill, covered, for 8 hours.
Yield: 8 servings.*

Beans for a Crowd

10 slices bacon, cut into pieces ▪ 1½ cups chopped onions
1 (15-ounce) can lima beans ▪ 1 (15-ounce) can kidney beans
1 (15-ounce) can Great Northern beans
1 (15-ounce) can pinto beans ▪ ¼ cup honey
3 tablespoons cider vinegar
2 teaspoons ground cumin ▪ 2 teaspoons dried oregano
2 teaspoons dry mustard ▪ Freshly ground pepper to taste
Salt to taste ▪ 1 red bell pepper, chopped
1 yellow bell pepper, chopped ▪ 1 green bell pepper, chopped
2 (10-ounce) packages frozen corn ▪ 2 ribs celery, diced
1 (28-ounce) can plum tomatoes, drained, chopped

*Crisp-fry bacon in large skillet; remove and crumble bacon, reserving
drippings in skillet. Add onions to drippings; cook over low heat until soft, but
not brown. Drain beans, reserving liquid; combine liquids. Stir 1 cup bean
liquid, honey, vinegar and seasonings into onions. Add bacon and remaining
ingredients; mix well. Pour into 11x15-inch baking dish. Bake at 350 degrees
for 1½ hours or until thickened and bubbly.
Yield: 12 servings.*

Baked Cabbage

1 medium head cabbage
Salt to taste
¼ cup finely chopped green bell pepper
¼ cup finely chopped onion
¼ cup butter or margarine
¼ cup flour ▪ ¼ teaspoon salt
⅛ teaspoon pepper ▪ 2 cups milk
½ cup shredded Cheddar cheese
¾ cup Thousand Island salad dressing

Cut cabbage into 8 wedges. Place in large saucepan with a small amount of water and salt. Bring to a boil over medium heat. Cook, covered, for 12 minutes or until tender; drain. Place in 9x13-inch baking dish. Sauté green pepper and onion in butter in skillet just until tender but not brown. Stir in flour, salt and pepper. Cook for 1 to 2 minutes, stirring frequently. Stir in milk and cheese gradually. Cook until thickened, stirring constantly. Spoon over cabbage. Bake at 375 degrees for 20 minutes. Spoon salad dressing over sauce layer. Bake for 5 minutes longer.
Yield: 6 servings.

French-Fried Cauliflower

1 head cauliflower
Salt to taste
1 cup bread crumbs
1 tablespoon grated Parmesan cheese
1 clove of garlic, minced
2 tablespoons chopped parsley
2 tablespoons chopped celery leaves
1 teaspoon salt ▪ Pepper to taste
2 eggs, beaten ▪ Vegetable oil for frying

Cook cauliflower in boiling salted water until tender-crisp; drain and separate into florets. Combine bread crumbs, cheese, garlic, parsley, celery, 1 teaspoon salt and pepper in bowl; mix well. Dip cauliflowerets into eggs; coat with bread crumb mixture. Fry in hot oil in skillet until golden brown; drain.
Yield: 6 servings.

Oven-Fried Eggplant

1 medium eggplant
1/2 cup cracker crumbs
1/4 cup Parmesan cheese
1 cup mayonnaise

Cut eggplant into 1/2-inch slices. Peel each slice. Combine cracker crumbs and Parmesan cheese in shallow bowl; mix well. Spread eggplant slices 1 side at a time with mayonnaise. Dip in crumb mixture; place in single layer in shallow baking pan. Bake at 425 degrees for 15 minutes or until brown and tender; do not turn slices.
Yield: 6 servings.

Vegetarian Eggplant

3 medium eggplant
8 ounces mushrooms, chopped
2 cloves of garlic, minced
1 cup chopped onion
Salt and pepper to taste
3 tablespoons butter or margarine
1 1/2 cups cottage cheese
1 cup cooked brown rice
1 cup grated Cheddar cheese
1/2 teaspoon thyme
Several drops of Tabasco sauce
1/4 cup toasted sunflower kernels
Paprika to taste
1/4 cup chopped fresh parsley

Slice eggplant lengthwise. Scoop out centers, leaving 1/4-inch shells. Reserve and chop centers. Sauté reserved eggplant with mushrooms, garlic, onion, salt and pepper in butter in skillet until onion is tender. Stir in cottage cheese, rice, Cheddar cheese, thyme, Tabasco sauce and sunflower kernels. Stuff eggplant shells with mixture; sprinkle with paprika and parsley. Arrange in buttered baking dish. Bake at 350 degrees for 40 minutes.
Yield: 6 servings.

Side Dishes • Breads

Old-Time Okra

1 pound fresh okra
1 green bell pepper, sliced into rings
$3/4$ teaspoon salt
3 large tomatoes
1 teaspoon sugar
$3/4$ teaspoon salt
5 or 6 slices bacon

Blanch whole okra pods in boiling water in saucepan for 1 minute; drain. Plunge into cold water in bowl. Drain well. Slice okra. Discard caps. Layer okra slices and green pepper rings in 6x10-inch baking dish. Sprinkle with $3/4$ teaspoon salt. Peel and slice tomatoes. Arrange tomato slices over okra and green pepper. Sprinkle with sugar and $3/4$ teaspoon salt. Top with bacon slices. Bake at 400 degrees for $1^1/4$ hours or until bacon is cooked through.
Yield: 6 servings.

To avoid breaking nutmeats, warm the nuts in their shells in a moderate oven. When the shells are then cracked, the nuts will come out whole and the skins can be easily loosened.

Onion Pie

1 cup coarsely crumbled saltine crackers
$1/2$ cup melted butter
$2^1/2$ cups thickly sliced Vidalia onions or other onions
2 tablespoons butter
8 ounces sliced Swiss cheese
1 teaspoon salt
Pepper to taste
$1^1/2$ cups milk
3 eggs, beaten

Mix cracker crumbs and $1/2$ cup melted butter in bowl. Press crumb mixture into 9-inch pie plate. Fry onions in 2 tablespoons butter in skillet until translucent. Cover bottom of pie plate with onions and top with cheese, salt and pepper. Scald milk and remove from heat. Stir a small amount of hot milk into beaten eggs; stir eggs into hot milk. Pour milk mixture over layers in pie plate. Bake at 350 degrees for 40 to 45 minutes or until brown.
Yield: 6 servings.

Potatoes Romanoff

6 large potatoes, peeled
2 cups large dry curd cottage cheese
1 cup sour cream
2 cloves of garlic, minced
1 teaspoon salt
3 scallions, finely chopped
1 cup shredded Cheddar cheese
1/8 teaspoon paprika

Cook potatoes in water in saucepan until tender. Drain; cut into cubes. Combine potatoes, cottage cheese, sour cream, garlic, salt and scallions in large bowl; mix well. Spoon into greased 2 1/2-quart baking dish. Sprinkle with cheese and paprika. Bake at 350 degrees for 30 minutes.
Yield: 8 servings.

Make-Ahead Mashed Potatoes

8 large potatoes
1 medium onion, chopped
1/2 cup margarine
8 ounces cream cheese, softened
1/2 cup sour cream
1 egg, beaten
Salt and pepper to taste
2 to 4 tablespoons butter or margarine
Paprika to taste

Peel and cut potatoes into thick slices. Place in large saucepan with onion and enough water to cover. Bring to a boil; reduce heat. Simmer for 20 minutes or until tender; drain. Combine with margarine, cream cheese, sour cream, egg, salt and pepper in mixer bowl. Beat at high speed until smooth. Spoon into greased 2-quart baking dish. Dot with butter; sprinkle with paprika. Bake at 350 degrees for 30 to 35 minutes or until heated through. May make up to 2 to 3 days ahead of time and refrigerate until ready to bake.
Yield: 8 to 10 servings.

Fiesta Rice

2 cups uncooked white rice
1 (15-ounce) can black beans, drained, rinsed
1 (15-ounce) can yellow corn, drained, rinsed
1 large red bell pepper, chopped
1 (4-ounce) can chopped green chiles
1/2 cup chopped green onions
1/2 cup chopped fresh cilantro ▪ 1/2 cup chopped black olives
1/2 cup chopped green olives
1/4 cup fresh orange juice
2 tablespoons lime juice ▪ 2 tablespoons olive oil
2 teaspoons ground cumin
1/2 teaspoon chili powder ▪ 1 teaspoon salt

Cook rice using package directions. Spoon into large bowl and fluff with fork. Cool to room temperature. Add beans, corn, bell pepper, green chiles, green onions, cilantro and olives. Add orange juice, lime juice, olive oil, cumin, chili powder and salt and toss lightly. Store, covered, for up to 2 days in the refrigerator. Serve chilled or at room temperature.
Yield: 12 servings.

Rice with Pine Nuts

1/4 cup pine nuts ▪ 3 tablespoons minced onion
1 clove of garlic, minced ▪ 2 1/2 tablespoons butter
1 cup uncooked rice
1 1/2 cups chicken broth ▪ 2 sprigs of parsley
1/4 teaspoon thyme ▪ 1/2 bay leaf
1/8 teaspoon cayenne

Place pine nuts in large baking pan. Bake at 325 degrees for 10 minutes or until toasted, stirring after 5 minutes. Sauté onion and garlic in butter in large skillet until tender. Stir in rice. Add chicken broth and mix well. Stir in parsley, thyme, bay leaf and cayenne. Bring to a boil; reduce heat to low. Simmer, covered, for 20 to 25 minutes or until broth has been absorbed. Remove bay leaf. Stir in pine nuts. Spoon into serving dish.
Yield: 4 servings.

Spinach Roc

2 or 3 fresh tomatoes, thickly sliced
2 (10-ounce) packages frozen spinach, cooked, drained
1½ cups herb-seasoned stuffing mix
6 eggs, beaten
1 teaspoon salt
1 tablespoon minced onion
½ cup grated Parmesan cheese
Pepper to taste
Garlic powder to taste
½ cup margarine
Bread crumbs

*Line bottom of greased 9x9-inch baking pan with tomato slices.
Combine spinach, stuffing mix, eggs, salt, onion, Parmesan cheese,
pepper and garlic powder in large bowl; mix well. Spoon over tomato
slices. Bake, uncovered, at 350 degrees for 30 minutes. Dot with
margarine and sprinkle with bread crumbs; serve hot.
Yield: 6 to 8 servings.*

Fresh Peach and Squash Casserole

2½ cups sliced peeled yellow or zucchini squash
1 cup sliced fresh peaches
2 tablespoons brown sugar
Salt to taste
2½ tablespoons butter

*Alternate layers of squash and peaches in greased 2-quart casserole.
Sprinkle with brown sugar and salt. Dot with butter. Bake, covered, at 350
degrees for 45 to 60 minutes or until squash is tender.
Yield: 4 servings.*

Squash with Praline Topping

2 (12-ounce) packages frozen squash
1/4 cup butter or margarine
1 teaspoon salt
Dash of pepper
2 eggs, beaten
1/3 cup packed light brown sugar
1/2 teaspoon cinnamon
1/2 cup chopped pecans

Combine squash, butter, salt and pepper in saucepan. Heat over low heat until squash is completely thawed, stirring frequently. Add gradually to beaten eggs in large bowl; mix well. Pour into greased 1-quart casserole. Combine brown sugar, cinnamon and pecans in bowl; sprinkle over squash. Bake at 350 degrees for 30 minutes.
Yield: 6 servings.

The pecan has a fat content of over 70 percent, more than any other nut.

Tomatoes Stuffed with Zucchini

6 medium tomatoes
Salt and pepper to taste
6 medium unpeeled zucchini, thinly sliced
1 1/2 teaspoons dried basil leaves
1/4 cup olive oil
2 cloves of garlic, pressed
2 tablespoons finely chopped fresh parsley
2 tablespoons butter
1 tablespoon finely chopped fresh parsley

Cut tops from tomatoes and scoop out pulp. Sprinkle with salt and pepper; invert to drain. Stir-fry zucchini and basil in olive oil in large skillet over medium-high heat for 4 to 5 minutes. Remove to drain on paper towel; sprinkle with salt and pepper. Sauté garlic and 2 tablespoons parsley in butter in same skillet for 2 minutes. Return zucchini to skillet; mix well. Spoon into tomato shells; sprinkle with 1 tablespoon parsley. Place in greased baking dish. Bake at 375 degrees for 15 minutes.
Yield: 6 servings.

Good Southern Biscuits

2 teaspoons confectioners' sugar
2 teaspoons baking powder
2 cups self-rising flour
1/3 cup shortening
1 cup buttermilk

Sift confectioners' sugar, baking powder and flour into bowl. Cut in shortening until crumbly. Add buttermilk, stirring just until moistened. Roll dough 1/2 inch thick. Cut with biscuit cutter. Place on greased baking sheet. Bake at 450 degrees for 12 to 15 minutes or until golden brown.
Yield: 12 servings.

Herbed Sour Cream Biscuits

4 cups flour
5 teaspoons baking powder
1/2 teaspoon baking soda
2 teaspoons dillweed
1 teaspoon dried basil
3/4 teaspoon salt
1 teaspoon pepper
1/2 teaspoon dried thyme leaves
1/2 cup butter or margarine
8 ounces sour cream
1 cup milk

Sift flour, baking powder, baking soda, dillweed, basil, salt, pepper and thyme into large bowl. Cut in butter until crumbly. Make well in center. Add sour cream and milk; mix well with wooden spoon. Roll dough 1/2-inch thick on lightly floured surface; cut with 2-inch biscuit cutter. Place on lightly greased baking sheet. Bake at 450 degrees for 15 to 18 minutes or until golden brown.
Yield: 18 servings.

Side Dishes • Breads

Cheddar and Sour Cream Corn Bread

^{1}/$_2$ cup margarine ▪ 1^1/$_2$ cups cornmeal
^{1}/$_3$ cup flour
4 teaspoons baking powder
^{1}/$_2$ teaspoon salt ▪ 2 eggs, beaten
1 cup sour cream
1 (17-ounce) can cream-style corn
^{1}/$_4$ to ^{1}/$_2$ cup grated onion
^{1}/$_2$ cup shredded Cheddar cheese

*Heat margarine in 9x13-inch baking dish in 375-degree oven until
melted. Combine cornmeal, flour, baking powder and salt in bowl; mix well.
Stir in eggs, sour cream, corn, onion and melted margarine. Spoon into
prepared baking dish. Bake for 40 minutes or until light brown. Sprinkle with
cheese. Let stand in oven until cheese melts. Cut into 1^1/$_2$-inch squares.
May add 3 tablespoons milk for thinner consistency.
Yield: 28 servings.*

Onion Corn Bread

1 sweet Spanish onion, sliced
^{1}/$_4$ cup butter
1 cup sour cream
^{1}/$_4$ teaspoon salt
^{1}/$_4$ teaspoon dillweed
1 cup shredded sharp Cheddar cheese
1^1/$_2$ cups corn muffin mix
1 egg, beaten ▪ ^{1}/$_3$ cup milk
2 drops of Tabasco sauce
1 cup cream-style corn

*Sauté onion in butter in medium skillet over low heat until tender. Cool slightly.
Stir in sour cream, salt, dillweed and half the cheese. Combine muffin mix, egg,
milk and Tabasco sauce in medium bowl and beat until well mixed. Stir in corn.
Spoon into greased 8x8-inch baking pan. Spoon onion mixture over batter and
top with remaining cheese. Bake at 425 degrees for 25 to 30 minutes or until
golden brown. Cut into squares and serve warm.
Yield: 9 servings.*

When using chopped
nuts in batter or
dough, toss the nuts
with a small amount
of the flour called for
in the recipe.
They will be more
evenly distributed in
the mixture.

Spinach Spoon Bread

1 (10-ounce) package frozen chopped spinach, thawed, drained
2 eggs, lightly beaten
1 (8-ounce) can cream-style corn
1 cup sour cream
1/2 cup melted butter
1/4 teaspoon salt
1 (8-ounce) package corn muffin mix
1/2 cup shredded Cheddar cheese

*Combine spinach, eggs, corn, sour cream, butter and salt in bowl; mix
well. Add corn muffin mix; mix well. Pour into greased 8-inch-round
baking dish. Bake at 350 degrees for 30 to 35 minutes or until corn bread
tests done. Sprinkle cheese on top. Bake until cheese melts. This may
also be served as a vegetable side dish.
Yield: 6 servings.*

Jonathan Apple Bread

2 cups sugar
1 cup vegetable oil ▪ 4 eggs, beaten
2 teaspoons vanilla extract
4 cups chopped Jonathan apples
1 cup raisins
1 cup chopped pecans ▪ 2²/₃ cups flour
1 1/2 teaspoons baking soda
1/2 teaspoon salt
2 teaspoons cinnamon
1 teaspoon ground cloves
1 tablespoon sugar

*Mix 2 cups sugar and oil in large mixer bowl. Add eggs and vanilla; mix well.
Stir in apples, raisins and pecans. Add mixture of flour, baking soda, salt,
cinnamon and cloves; mix well. Pour into 5 greased 3x6-inch loaf pans. Tap to
settle. Bake at 325 degrees for 20 minutes. Sprinkle 1 tablespoon sugar over
top of loaves. Bake for 30 to 40 minutes longer. Cool in pans for 10 minutes.
Remove to wire racks to cool completely.
Yield: 5 loaves.*

Side Dishes • Breads

Artichoke Bread

1 long loaf French bread
1/3 cup margarine
1/2 teaspoon garlic powder
2 teaspoons sesame seeds
1 (14-ounce) can artichoke hearts, drained, chopped
1 cup shredded Monterey Jack cheese
3/4 cup grated Parmesan cheese
1/2 cup sour cream
1/2 cup shredded Cheddar cheese

Slice bread loaf lengthwise into halves. Scoop out center of each half, leaving 1-inch shell. Crumble bread from center; set aside. Melt margarine in skillet. Stir in garlic powder and sesame seeds. Cook until light brown, stirring constantly. Stir in artichokes, Monterey Jack cheese, Parmesan cheese and sour cream. Add crumbled bread; mix well. Spoon into bread shells. Place on baking sheet. Bake, covered with foil, at 350 degrees for 25 minutes; remove foil. Sprinkle with Cheddar cheese. Bake until cheese melts. Cut into slices.
Yield: 24 servings.

Sour Cream Banana Bread

1 cup sugar
1/2 cup butter or margarine, softened
2 eggs ▪ 1 1/2 cups flour
1 teaspoon baking soda
1/2 teaspoon salt
1 cup mashed bananas ▪ 1/2 cup sour cream
1 teaspoon vanilla extract
1/2 cup chopped walnuts
1/2 cup chocolate chips

Cream sugar, butter and eggs in mixer bowl until light and fluffy. Add mixture of flour, baking soda and salt, beating until blended. Stir in bananas, sour cream and vanilla. Fold in walnuts and chocolate chips. Spoon into buttered 5x9-inch loaf pan. Bake at 350 degrees for 1 hour. Cool in pan on wooden board for 10 minutes. Invert onto wire rack to cool completely.
Yield: 12 servings.

White Chocolate Banana Bread

Softened butter or margarine
Wheat germ ▪ 2³⁄₄ cups unsifted flour
1¹⁄₄ teaspoons baking soda
1 teaspoon salt ▪ 1¹⁄₂ cups sugar
1 cup butter or margarine, melted
2 eggs ▪ 3 tablespoons apple juice
1 teaspoon vanilla extract
2 cups mashed bananas
6 ounces white chocolate, cut into ¹⁄₄-inch squares
3¹⁄₂ ounces shredded coconut
1 cup chopped walnuts (optional)
Sesame seeds (optional)

Butter two 6-cup loaf pans; dust with wheat germ. Mix flour, baking soda and salt in bowl. Cream sugar and 1 cup butter in mixer bowl. Add eggs, apple juice and vanilla; beat for 5 minutes. Mix in bananas. Add flour mixture gradually, stirring until well mixed but still lumpy. Stir in white chocolate, coconut and walnuts. Pour into prepared pans; smooth tops. Sprinkle generously with sesame seeds. Bake at 350 degrees for 55 minutes. Cover pans with foil to prevent overbrowning; bake for 20 minutes longer. Cool in pans for 10 minutes; remove to wire rack to cool completely.
Yield: 24 servings.

Lemon Loaf

1¹⁄₂ cups sugar
6 tablespoons butter, softened ▪ 2 eggs, beaten
Grated peel of 1 lemon
1¹⁄₂ cups flour ▪ 1 teaspoon baking powder
¹⁄₄ teaspoon salt ▪ ¹⁄₂ cup milk ▪ Juice of 1 lemon

Cream 1 cup of sugar and butter in mixer bowl until light and fluffy. Add eggs and lemon peel and mix well. Sift flour, baking powder and salt together. Add alternately with milk, mixing well after each addition. Pour into greased and floured loaf pan. Bake at 350 degrees for 1 hour. Mix lemon juice with remaining ¹⁄₂ cup sugar in bowl. Spoon over loaf. Cool in pan on wire rack.
Yield: 10 servings.

Side Dishes • Breads

Olive Bread

5 cups flour
2¹/₂ tablespoons baking powder
²/₃ cup sugar
¹/₂ teaspoon dried thyme
¹/₂ teaspoon salt ▪ 2 eggs
2 cups milk
2 cups sliced stuffed green olives
¹/₄ cup chopped pimento
2 cups chopped walnuts

Sift flour, baking powder, sugar, thyme and salt into large bowl. Beat eggs lightly in bowl. Add milk; beat until blended. Stir mixture into dry ingredients until blended. Fold in olives, pimento and walnuts. Pour into two greased 5x9-inch loaf pans. Bake at 350 degrees for 55 to 60 minutes or until bread tests done. Cool in pans for 5 minutes. Invert onto wire racks to cool completely.
Yield: 24 servings.

One pound of walnuts in the shell will yield about two cups of shelled nuts.

Orange Slice Bread

2 cups chopped dates
1 cup boiling coffee
³/₄ cup shortening
2 eggs ▪ 2 cups sugar
4 cups flour
1 teaspoon baking soda
1 teaspoon salt
1 cup buttermilk
1 package candy orange slices, cut up
1 cup chopped nuts

Soak dates in boiling coffee in bowl; let cool. Dates will soak up coffee. Beat shortening in mixer bowl until creamy. Beat in eggs and sugar. Combine flour, baking soda and salt in bowl. Add to creamed mixture alternately with buttermilk, stirring after each addition. Add dates, orange slices and nuts; stir until blended. Pour into 2 greased 5x9-inch loaf pans. Bake at 350 degrees for 1¹/₄ hours. Cool in pans for 10 minutes; remove to racks to cool completely.
Yield: 16 servings.

Glazed Poppy Seed Bread

3 cups flour
2¼ cups sugar ▪ 1½ teaspoons salt
1½ teaspoons baking powder ▪ 3 eggs ▪ 1½ cups milk
1⅛ cups vegetable oil ▪ 1½ tablespoons poppy seeds
2 teaspoons vanilla extract
2 teaspoons almond extract ▪ 2 teaspoons butter flavoring
¾ cup sugar ▪ ¼ cup orange juice

*Combine flour, 2¼ cups sugar, salt and baking powder in large mixer bowl. Add eggs, milk and oil; mix well. Stir in poppy seeds, 1½ teaspoons vanilla, 1½ teaspoons almond extract and 1½ teaspoons butter flavoring; mix well. Pour into 5 small nonstick loaf pans. Bake at 350 degrees for 35 to 40 minutes. Spread mixture of ¾ cup sugar, orange juice and remaining ½ teaspoon vanilla, ½ teaspoon almond extract and ½ teaspoon butter flavoring over warm bread.
Yield: 5 loaves.*

Pumpkin Swirl Bread

1¾ cups flour ▪ 1½ cups sugar ▪ 1 teaspoon baking soda
1 teaspoon cinnamon ▪ ½ teaspoon salt
¼ teaspoon ground nutmeg
1 cup canned pumpkin ▪ ½ cup melted margarine
1 egg, beaten ▪ ⅓ cup water
8 ounces cream cheese, softened
¼ cup sugar ▪ 1 egg, beaten

*Combine flour, sugar, baking soda, cinnamon, salt and nutmeg in large mixer bowl; mix well. Add mixture of pumpkin, margarine, 1 egg and water; mix just until moistened. Reserve 2 cups pumpkin mixture. Divide remaining batter evenly into 2 greased and floured 5x9-inch loaf pans. Beat cream cheese, sugar and 1 egg in bowl until smooth. Spread half the cream cheese mixture over batter in each pan. Pour reserved pumpkin mixture over the top. Swirl through layers with a knife to marbelize. Bake at 350 degrees for 1 hour and 10 minutes or until wooden pick inserted in center comes out clean. Cool in pans for 5 minutes. Remove to wire racks to cool completely.
Yield: 2 loaves.*

Raspberry Bread

2 cups flour ▪ 1 cup sugar
1½ teaspoons baking powder
½ teaspoon baking soda ▪ 1 teaspoon salt
¼ cup shortening ▪ ¾ cup orange juice
1 tablespoon orange peel
1 egg, beaten ▪ ½ cup chopped nuts
2 cups fresh or frozen whole raspberries

Sift flour, sugar, baking powder, baking soda and salt in large bowl. Cut in shortening until mixture resembles coarse cornmeal. Combine orange juice and orange peel with egg in bowl. Pour into dry ingredients, mixing just enough to moisten. Fold in nuts and raspberries. Pour into greased 5x9-inch loaf pan, spreading corners and sides slightly higher than center. Bake at 350 degrees for 1 hour or until wooden pick inserted in center comes out clean. Cool in pan for 10 minutes. Invert onto wire rack to cool completely.
Yield: 10 to 12 servings.

Strawberry Walnut Bread

1 cup butter or margarine, softened ▪ 1½ cups sugar
1 teaspoon vanilla extract ▪ ¼ teaspoon lemon extract ▪ 4 eggs
3 cups flour ▪ 1 teaspoon salt ▪ 1 teaspoon cream of tartar
½ teaspoon baking soda ▪ 1 cup strawberry jam
½ cup sour cream ▪ ½ cup chopped walnuts
3 ounces cream cheese, softened
2 tablespoons strawberry jam

Cream butter, sugar, vanilla and lemon extract in large mixer bowl until light and fluffy. Add eggs 1 at a time, beating well after each addition. Add mixture of flour, salt, cream of tartar and baking soda alternately with mixture of 1 cup jam and sour cream, mixing well after each addition. Stir in walnuts. Pour into 2 greased and floured 5x9-inch loaf pans. Bake at 350 degrees for 50 minutes or until wooden pick inserted in center comes out clean. Cool in pans for 10 minutes. Remove to wire racks to cool completely. Combine cream cheese and 2 tablespoons strawberry jam in bowl; mix well. Serve strawberry cream cheese with thinly sliced strawberry bread.
Yield: 2 loaves.

Nutty Zucchini and Honey Loaves

4 eggs
1 cup vegetable oil ▪ 2 cups sugar
2 cups grated zucchini
2 teaspoons vanilla extract
¾ cup honey ▪ 3 cups flour
1 teaspoon salt
1 teaspoon baking powder
1 teaspoon baking soda
1 tablespoon cinnamon
1 cup chopped nuts
½ cup shredded coconut

Beat eggs in mixer bowl until light and foamy. Add oil, sugar, zucchini, vanilla and honey; mix well. Sift flour, salt, baking powder, baking soda and cinnamon together. Add to mixture; beat well. Fold in nuts and coconut. Pour into 2 greased 5x9-inch loaf pans. Bake at 325 degrees for 1 hour or until loaves test done. Invert onto wire racks to cool.
Yield: 24 servings.

Roast shelled nuts in the microwave on High for 6 to 10 minutes, stirring frequently.

Breakfast Muffins

1½ cups whole wheat flour
1½ cups rolled oats
1 cup all-purpose flour ▪ ⅔ cup sugar
⅓ cup wheat germ
2 teaspoons baking soda
2 teaspoons cinnamon
1 teaspoon salt ▪ 3 eggs, lightly beaten
1 (8-ounce) can crushed pineapple
2 cups mashed bananas
½ cup vegetable oil

Combine whole wheat flour with oats, flour, sugar, wheat germ, baking soda, cinnamon and salt in large bowl. Make a well in center. Add eggs, pineapple, bananas and oil. Stir just until moistened. Spoon into greased and floured muffin cups. Bake at 350 degrees for 20 minutes.
Yield: 24 servings.

Side Dishes • Breads

Creole Corn Muffins

1¼ cups flour ▪ 2 tablespoons cornmeal
1 tablespoon baking powder
½ teaspoon salt ▪ ⅛ teaspoon red pepper
⅓ cup shredded Cheddar cheese
1 tablespoon chopped green bell pepper
1 tablespoon chopped onion
1 tablespoon chopped pimento ▪ 1 egg, beaten
⅓ cup vegetable oil ▪ ¾ cup milk

Combine flour, cornmeal, baking powder, salt and red pepper in large bowl. Add cheese, green pepper, onion and pimento; mix well. Beat egg with oil and milk in small bowl. Add to flour mixture; mix just until moistened. Spoon into greased muffin cups. Bake at 400 degrees for 25 minutes or until golden brown. Yield: 8 servings.

Orange Blossom Muffins

1 egg, lightly beaten ▪ ¼ cup sugar
½ cup orange juice ▪ 2 tablespoons vegetable oil
2 cups baking mix ▪ ½ cup orange marmalade
½ cup chopped pecans ▪ Spicy Topping

Combine egg, sugar, orange juice and oil in medium bowl. Add baking mix; beat for 30 seconds. Stir in marmalade and pecans. Fill greased or paper-lined muffin cups ⅔ full. Sprinkle with Spicy Topping. Bake at 400 degrees for 20 to 25 minutes or until golden brown. Yield: 12 servings.

Spicy Topping

¼ cup sugar ▪ 1½ tablespoons flour
½ teaspoon cinnamon ▪ ¼ teaspoon nutmeg
1 tablespoon butter or margarine

Combine sugar, flour, cinnamon and nutmeg in small bowl; mix well. Cut in butter with fork until mixture is crumbly. Yield: 6½ tablespoons.

Apple Sticky Buns

2 to 3 apples, sliced
1 (10-count) can biscuits
1/2 cup packed light brown sugar
2 teaspoons cinnamon
1 teaspoon nutmeg
1/2 cup melted butter or margarine

Arrange apple slices in bottom of greased 8x8-inch baking dish. Separate biscuits. Coat with mixture of brown sugar, cinnamon and nutmeg. Arrange over apple slices. Drizzle with butter. Bake at 350 degrees for 20 to 30 minutes or until golden brown. Remove to serving plate immediately.
Yield: 6 to 8 servings.

Drop Doughnuts

1 cup sugar
Dash of salt
1 tablepoon baking powder
3 cups flour
Dash of nutmeg
2 eggs
1 cup milk
1 teaspoon vanilla extract
Vegetable oil for frying
Confectioners' sugar

Combine sugar, salt, baking powder, flour and nutmeg in bowl; mix well. Combine eggs, milk and vanilla in bowl; mix well. Stir into dry ingredients. Drop batter by spoonfuls into hot oil in skillet or deep fryer. Cook until golden brown. Drain on paper towels. Roll in confectioners' sugar.
Yield: 6 servings.

Side Dishes • Breads

Oven Pancakes

1½ tablespoons vegetable oil
½ cup flour
½ cup milk
2 eggs
1 tablespoon vanilla extract
2 tablespoons sugar
1 small banana, chopped

Pour oil into large pie plate; swirl around. Place in preheated 450-degree oven. Combine flour, milk, eggs, vanilla and sugar in mixer bowl; beat for 1 minute. Add banana. Pour into hot pie plate. Bake for 20 minutes. Turn onto bread board. Cut into halves.
Yield: 2 servings.

1 cup sliced almonds
weighs 3¼ ounces
1 cup slivered almonds
weighs 4½ ounces
1 cup whole almonds
weighs 5 ounces

Light and Fluffy Pancakes

1 cup plus 2 tablespoons flour
1 tablespoon sugar
1 teaspoon baking powder
½ teaspoon baking soda
2 tablespoons plus 2 teaspoons soft whipped margarine, melted
1 cup vanilla yogurt
2 eggs
2 teaspoons vanilla extract
¼ cup water
1 cup fresh or frozen blueberries

Combine flour, sugar, baking powder and baking soda in bowl; mix well. Combine margarine, yogurt, eggs, vanilla and water in bowl; mix well. Add dry ingredients; mix well. Add additional water if needed. Fold in blueberries. Spray griddle with nonstick cooking spray. Drop batter by spoonfuls onto hot griddle. Bake until bubbles form on top. Turn and bake until brown on bottom.
Yield: 12 pancakes.

Gingerbread Waffles

1 cup all-purpose flour ▪ ¾ cup whole wheat or oat bran flour
1 tablespoon baking powder
¼ teaspoon salt ▪ ½ teaspoon ginger
¼ teaspoon cloves ▪ 2 eggs
1⅓ cups milk ▪ ½ cup vegetable oil ▪ ⅓ cup molasses

Mix all-purpose flour, whole wheat flour, baking powder, salt, ginger and cloves together. Combine eggs, milk, oil and molasses in medium bowl; whisk until blended. Add flour mixture; mix just until moistened. Batter will be lumpy. Ladle onto preheated waffle iron sprayed with nonstick cooking spray. Bake using manufacturer's directions. Serve warm with syrup or apricot jam.
Yield: 10 to 12 (4-inch) waffles.

Orange Pecan Waffles

2 cups waffle mix ▪ 1½ cups water
1 tablespoon canola oil
1 cup chopped pecans
Grated peel of 1 orange ▪ Orange Sauce

Combine waffle mix, water and oil in bowl. Beat with rotary beater until fairly smooth. Stir in pecans and orange peel. Ladle onto preheated waffle iron. Bake using manufacturer's directions. Remove to serving plates. Spoon Orange Sauce over top.
Yield: 4 servings.

Orange Sauce

½ cup butter ▪ 1 cup sugar
2 eggs ▪ 1 tablespoon boiling water ▪ ½ cup orange juice
2 tablespoons lemon juice ▪ 2 tablespoons grated orange peel

Combine butter, sugar and eggs in saucepan; mix well. Stir in boiling water. Cook over medium heat until butter is melted. Add orange juice, lemon juice and orange peel gradually, mixing well. Cook until sauce is consistency of heavy cream, stirring constantly.
Yield: 2½ cups.

Side Dishes • Breads

Desserts

Delicious Banana Pudding

1 (14-ounce) can sweetened condensed milk
1 1/2 cups cold water
1 (4-ounce) package vanilla instant pudding mix
2 cups whipped topping
3 medium bananas, sliced
1/2 cup lemon juice
36 vanilla wafers

*Combine condensed milk, cold water and pudding mix in mixer bowl; mix
well. Chill in freezer for 5 minutes. Fold in whipped topping. Combine bananas
and lemon juice in bowl, stirring gently to coat bananas; drain. Alternate
layers of pudding, vanilla wafers and banana slices in 6x8-inch dish until all
are used, ending with pudding. Chill until serving time.*
Yield: 8 servings.

Blueberry Buckle

2 cups flour
3/4 cup sugar
1/4 cup shortening
1 egg
1/2 cup milk
2 teaspoons baking powder
1/2 teaspoon salt
2 cups blueberries
1/2 cup sugar
1/3 cup flour
1/2 teaspoon cinnamon
1/4 cup butter

*Combine 2 cups flour, 3/4 cup sugar, shortening, egg, milk, baking powder
and salt in bowl; mix well. Fold in blueberries. Spoon into greased and floured
9x9-inch baking pan. Combine 1/2 cup sugar, 1/3 cup flour, cinnamon and
butter in bowl. Mix until crumbly. Sprinkle over batter. Bake at 375 degrees
for 45 to 50 minutes or until brown.*
Yield: 16 servings.

Chocolate Fudge Praline Cheesecake

1 cup graham cracker crumbs ▪ ¼ cup ground pecans
¼ cup melted margarine ▪ 3 tablespoons light brown sugar
½ teaspoon cinnamon ▪ 24 ounces cream cheese, softened
½ cup packed light brown sugar ▪ ½ cup sugar
2 tablespoons flour ▪ 3 eggs ▪ 1 cup sour cream
2 ounces unsweetened chocolate, melted
¼ cup packed light brown sugar
1 tablespoon melted margarine ▪ ½ cup chopped pecans

Combine graham cracker crumbs, ¼ cup pecans, ¼ cup margarine, 3 tablespoons brown sugar and cinnamon in bowl; mix until crumbly. Press over bottom and side of greased 9-inch springform pan. Bake at 350 degrees for 10 minutes. Cool completely. Combine cream cheese, ½ cup brown sugar, sugar and flour in mixer bowl; beat until smooth. Add eggs 1 at a time, mixing well after each addition. Add sour cream and chocolate; mix until blended. Spread over prepared crust. Bake at 425 degrees for 10 minutes. Reduce heat to 250 degrees. Sprinkle with mixture of ¼ cup brown sugar, 1 tablespoon margarine and ½ cup pecans on top. Bake for 45 minutes longer. Loosen from side of pan. Cool completely in pan before removing rim. Store in refrigerator.
Yield: 10 to 12 servings.

When chopping nuts for desserts in a blender or food processor, add 2 teaspoons of sugar to each ½ cup nuts to prevent forming a paste.

Company Cheesecake

1¾ cups cinnamon crisp graham cracker crumbs
¼ cup finely chopped walnuts ▪ 2 tablespoons sugar
⅓ cup butter, softened ▪ 3 eggs, beaten
16 ounces cream cheese, softened ▪ 1 cup sugar
¼ teaspoon salt ▪ 2 teaspoons vanilla extract
½ teaspoon almond extract ▪ 3 cups sour cream

Combine graham cracker crumbs, walnuts, 2 tablespoons sugar and butter in bowl; mix well. Press over bottom and side of 9-inch springform pan. Combine eggs, cream cheese, 1 cup sugar, salt and flavorings in mixer bowl, beating until blended. Add sour cream; mix well. Spoon into prepared pan. Bake at 375 degrees for 35 minutes or just until light brown and top cracks. Turn off oven. Let stand in oven with door slightly ajar until cool.
Yield: 12 servings.

Chocolate Mint Dessert

1 cup semisweet chocolate chips
1 cup miniature marshmallows
1 cup evaporated milk
$\frac{1}{2}$ cup butter or margarine
1 cup flour
$\frac{1}{4}$ cup packed brown sugar
$\frac{1}{2}$ cup chopped pecans
$\frac{1}{2}$ gallon peppermint or mint-chocolate chip ice cream, softened

Combine chocolate chips, marshmallows and evaporated milk in medium saucepan. Heat over low heat until chocolate chips are melted, stirring frequently. Remove from heat and let cool. Cut butter into flour with pastry blender in large bowl until mixture is crumbly. Stir in brown sugar and pecans. Press mixture over bottom of 10x14-inch baking sheet. Bake at 400 degrees for 10 to 12 minutes or until light brown. Crumble baked mixture and press over bottom of greased 8x8-inch baking pan, reserving 2 tablespoons for topping. Spread half the ice cream over the crumb crust. Top with half the chocolate mixture. Spread with remaining ice cream and chocolate mixture. Top with reserved crumbs. Freeze until firm.
Yield: 12 servings.

Granola Peaches and Ice Cream

1 (29-ounce) can peach halves, drained
2 tablespoons brown sugar
$\frac{2}{3}$ cup granola
$\frac{1}{4}$ cup packed brown sugar
3 tablespoons melted margarine
2 tablespoons chopped pecans
6 scoops vanilla ice cream

Place peach halves cut side up in baking dish. Sprinkle with 2 tablespoons brown sugar. Broil 5 inches from heat source for 2 to 3 minutes or until light brown. Combine granola, $\frac{1}{4}$ cup brown sugar, margarine and pecans in a small bowl; mix well. Sprinkle over peaches. Broil for 1 minute or until bubbly and brown. Place in dessert dishes. Add scoop of vanilla ice cream.
Yield: 6 servings.

Desserts

Milky Way Homemade Ice Cream

5 eggs, separated
2^1/$_2$ cups sugar
6 Milky Way candy bars, melted
1 cup milk, scalded
2 cups half-and-half
1 cup whipping cream
Milk

Beat egg whites in mixer bowl until stiff. Add beaten egg yolks and sugar; mix well. Mix candy into hot milk. Stir a small amount of hot mixture into egg mixture; stir egg mixture into hot mixture. Stir in half-and-half and whipping cream. Pour into ice cream freezer container. Add milk to fill line. Freeze, using manufacturer's instructions.
Yield: 1 gallon.

Baked-In Strawberry Shortcake

1^1/$_2$ cups flour
^{3}/$_4$ cup sugar
2 teaspoons baking powder
^{1}/$_2$ teaspoon salt
^{1}/$_2$ cup milk
1 egg
2 tablespoons melted butter or margarine
2^1/$_2$ cups chopped strawberries
^{1}/$_4$ cup butter or margarine, softened
Whipped cream

Sift 1 cup of flour, ^{1}/$_2$ cup of sugar, baking powder and salt into mixer bowl. Add milk, egg and melted butter. Beat at low speed for 2 minutes. Spoon into greased 8x8-inch baking pan. Top with strawberries. Combine remaining ^{1}/$_2$ cup flour, ^{1}/$_4$ cup sugar and ^{1}/$_4$ cup softened butter in small bowl, stirring until crumbly. Sprinkle over strawberries. Bake at 350 degrees for 35 to 40 minutes or until light brown. Top with whipped cream.
Yield: 9 servings.

Roast almonds by brushing 1/2 teaspoon melted butter, margarine, or peanut or vegetable oil over the surface of a shallow baking pan. Spread almonds in a single layer in the prepared pan. Roast at 300 degrees for 15 minutes or until they begin to brown, stirring frequently.

White Chocolate Mousse

12 ounces white chocolate ▪ 3/4 cup milk
1 envelope unflavored gelatin ▪ 1/4 cup milk
1 teaspoon vanilla extract ▪ 4 egg whites, at room temperature
2 cups whipping cream ▪ Dash of lemon juice
1 (10-ounce) package frozen raspberries ▪ 1 tablespoon apple juice

*Melt white chocolate in 3/4 cup milk in double boiler over hot but not boiling water; mix well. Remove from heat. Soften gelatin in 1/4 cup milk. Add to chocolate mixture; stir until smooth. Blend in vanilla. Beat egg whites until stiff peaks form. Fold gently 1/3 at a time into chocolate mixture. Whip cream until soft peaks form. Fold with lemon juice into chocolate mixture. Pour into serving bowl. Chill for several hours. Purée raspberries in blender. Strain to remove seeds. Blend in apple juice. Chill in refrigerator. Spoon sauce over mousse to serve.
Yield: 12 servings.*

Almond Joy Cake

2 cups sugar ▪ 2 cups flour ▪ 1 cup water ▪ 1/2 cup margarine
1/2 cup shortening ▪ 3 1/2 tablespoons baking cocoa ▪ 1/2 teaspoon salt
2 eggs ▪ 1/2 cup buttermilk ▪ 1 teaspoon vanilla extract
1 teaspoon baking soda ▪ 1 cup sugar
1 cup evaporated milk ▪ 24 large marshmallows
1 (7-ounce) package shredded coconut ▪ 1/2 cup margarine
1 (12-ounce) package semisweet chocolate chips
1 cup sliced almonds

*Mix 2 cups sugar and 2 cups flour in bowl. Mix water, 1/2 cup margarine, shortening and baking cocoa in saucepan; bring to a boil. Pour over sugar-flour mixture; mix well. Add next 5 ingredients; mix well. Pour into greased and floured 9x13-inch baking pan. Bake at 350 degrees for 40 minutes or until wooden pick inserted in center comes out clean. Mix 1 cup sugar, evaporated milk and marshmallows in saucepan. Cook until marshmallows are melted, stirring constantly. Add coconut; pour over hot cake. Melt 1/2 cup margarine and chocolate chips in saucepan; mix well. Add almonds; spread over top.
Yield: 18 to 24 servings.*

Desserts

Apple Skillet Cake

1½ cups flour
1 teaspoon baking soda
1 teaspoon salt
1 cup sugar
1 teaspoon cinnamon
½ teaspoon allspice
¾ cup vegetable oil
½ cup buttermilk
1 egg, slightly beaten
2 Granny Smith apples, peeled, sliced
1 teaspoon vanilla extract
1 cup chopped pecans

*Sift flour, baking soda, salt, sugar, cinnamon and allspice into bowl.
Add oil, buttermilk, egg, apples, vanilla and pecans; mix well.
Spoon into greased 9- or 10-inch cast-iron skillet. Bake at 350 degrees for
40 to 50 minutes or until cake tests done. Cool in skillet.
Yield: 12 servings.*

Chocolate Upside-Down Cake

1 cup packed light brown sugar
½ cup baking cocoa
2 cups water
12 to 14 marshmallows, quartered
1 (2-layer) package chocolate cake mix
½ cup chopped walnuts

*Combine brown sugar, baking cocoa, water and marshmallows in bowl and
mix well. Spread in greased 9x13-inch cake pan..Prepare cake mix using
package directions. Spoon over brown sugar mixture. Sprinkle with walnuts.
Bake at 350 degrees for 25 to 35 minutes or until cake tests done. Cool in
pan. Invert to serve. Serve with whipped cream or ice cream.
Yield: 12 servings.*

Chocolate Fudge Cake

1 cup butter or margarine
1 cup water
$^{1}/_{2}$ cup vegetable oil
1 teaspoon vanilla extract
5 tablespoons baking cocoa
2 cups flour
2 cups sugar
2 eggs
$^{1}/_{2}$ cup buttermilk
1 teaspoon baking soda
$^{1}/_{4}$ cup butter or margarine
6 tablespoons baking cocoa
2 tablespoons vegetable oil
7 tablespoons milk
Confectioners' sugar to taste

Combine 1 cup butter, water, $^{1}/_{2}$ cup oil, vanilla and 5 tablespoons baking cocoa in medium saucepan; mix well. Bring to a boil over medium heat. Add to mixture of flour and sugar in large bowl, stirring until blended. Add eggs 1 at a time, mixing after well after each addition. Add mixture of buttermilk and baking soda. Spoon into greased and floured 9x9-inch cake pan. Bake at 350 degrees for 35 minutes; do not overbake. Combine $^{1}/_{4}$ cup butter, 6 tablespoons baking cocoa, 2 tablespoons oil and milk in saucepan; mix well. Cook over low heat until butter melts, stirring constantly. Add enough confectioners' sugar to make of spreading consistency. Frost top of cake.
Yield: 9 servings.

Great-Grandmother's Gingerbread

2¹/₃ cups flour, sifted
1 teaspoon cinnamon
1 teaspoon ginger
¹/₂ teaspoon cloves
1¹/₂ teaspoons baking soda
¹/₂ teaspoon salt
¹/₂ cup butter or margarine, softened
¹/₂ cup sugar
1 egg, beaten
1 cup molasses
1 cup hot water
Lemon Sauce

Sift flour and next 5 ingredients together. Cream butter and sugar in mixer bowl until light and fluffy. Add egg; mix well. Add sifted dry ingredients and mixture of molasses and hot water alternately, mixing well after each addition. Spoon into 9x9-inch waxed-paper-lined cake pan. Bake at 350 degrees for 45 minutes. Serve warm with Lemon Sauce.
Yield: 16 servings.

Lemon Sauce

¹/₂ cup sugar
1 tablespoon cornstarch
1 cup boiling water
Salt to taste
2 tablespoons butter or margarine
2 tablespoons lemon juice
Nutmeg to taste
Grated lemon peel to taste

Combine sugar and cornstarch in top of double boiler. Stir in boiling water and salt. Cook over direct heat until thickened and clear, stirring constantly. Place pan over hot water. Cook for 20 minutes. Beat in butter and remaining ingredients.
Yield: 16 servings.

Lemon Poppy Seed Cake

4 egg whites ▪ ¹/₄ cup sugar
¹/₂ cup butter, softened ▪ 1¹/₄ cups sugar
¹/₄ cup milk ▪ 1 teaspoon lemon extract
2 cups flour ▪ 2 teaspoons baking powder
¹/₂ teaspoon salt ▪ ¹/₂ cup poppy seeds ▪ ³/₄ cup milk

*Beat egg whites in mixer bowl until soft peaks form. Add ¹/₄ cup sugar
gradually, beating until stiff peaks form. Set aside. Cream butter and 1¹/₄ cups
sugar in mixer bowl until light and fluffy. Add ¹/₄ cup milk and lemon extract;
beat until well blended. Add mixture of flour, baking powder, salt and
poppy seeds alternately with ³/₄ cup milk, beating well after each addition. Fold
in stiffly beaten egg whites gently. Pour into well greased and lightly floured
tube or bundt pan. Bake at 350 degrees for 1¹/₄ hours or until cake tests done.
Cool in pan for 5 minutes. Invert onto wire rack to cool completely. Frost with
favorite frosting or sprinkle with confectioners' sugar.
Yield: 16 servings.*

Six-Flavor Pound Cake

3 cups sugar ▪ ¹/₂ cup shortening
¹/₂ cup butter, softened
5 eggs, beaten ▪ 3 cups cake flour, sifted
1 teaspoon baking powder ▪ ¹/₄ teaspoon salt
1 cup milk ▪ 1 teaspoon orange extract
1 teaspoon lemon extract
1 teaspoon rum extract
1 teaspoon vanilla extract
1 teaspoon coconut extract
1 teaspoon butter flavoring

*Beat sugar, shortening and butter in mixer bowl until creamy. Add
eggs; mix well. Mix cake flour, baking powder and salt together. Add to
creamed mixture alternately with milk, mixing well after each addition.
Stir in flavorings. Spoon into greased and floured 10-inch tube pan.
Bake at 350 degrees for 1 hour. Glaze with your favorite icing if desired.
This cake freezes well for up to 2 months.
Yield: 20 servings.*

Golden Apricot Squares

²/₃ cup dried apricots, chopped
1 cup flour
¹/₄ cup confectioners' sugar
¹/₂ cup butter or margarine
2 eggs ▪ 1 cup sugar
¹/₄ cup lemon juice
¹/₂ teaspoon grated lemon peel
2 tablespoons flour
¹/₂ teaspoon baking powder
¹/₂ cup shredded coconut (optional)

Place apricots in saucepan with water to cover. Simmer over low heat for 10 minutes; drain. Combine 1 cup flour and confectioners' sugar in bowl. Cut in butter until crumbly. Press into greased 9x9-inch baking pan. Bake at 350 degrees for 20 to 25 minutes or until lightly browned. Beat eggs in mixer bowl until creamy. Beat in sugar, lemon juice and lemon peel. Add mixture of 2 tablespoons flour and baking powder; mix well. Stir in apricots and coconut. Spread over baked layer. Bake for 25 minutes. Cool. Sprinkle with confectioners' sugar. Cut into squares.
Yield: 30 servings.

Peanuts are high in niacin and important also for other B vitamins.

Christmas Candy

2 (1-pound) packages brown sugar
¹/₂ cup butter ▪ 1 cup evaporated milk
1 (7-ounce) jar marshmallow creme
2 (6-ounce) packages butterscotch chips
2¹/₂ cups coarsely chopped peanuts
1 teaspoon vanilla extract

Combine brown sugar, butter and evaporated milk in saucepan. Cook to 234 to 240 degrees on candy thermometer, soft-ball stage; remove from heat. Add marshmallow creme, beating for 8 minutes or until thick and creamy. Add butterscotch chips, peanuts and vanilla; mix well. Spoon into buttered 9x13-inch dish. Let stand until firm. Cut into bite-size pieces with warm sharp knife.
Yield: 100 servings.

Coconut Balls

1 cup creamy peanut butter
1 cup sifted confectioners' sugar
2 tablespoons melted margarine
1/2 cup chopped pecans
1 cup shredded coconut

*Combine peanut butter, confectioners' sugar, margarine and
pecans in bowl; mix well. Shape into 1/2-inch balls. Roll in coconut,
coating well. Chill in refrigerator.
Yield: 36 servings.*

Velveeta Fudge

8 ounces Velveeta cheese
1 cup butter
1 1/2 teaspoons vanilla extract
1/2 cup baking cocoa
2 (1-pound) packages confectioners' sugar
1/2 cup nuts

*Combine cheese and butter in large saucepan over low heat. Heat until
melted, stirring constantly; remove from heat. Add vanilla and baking cocoa;
blend well. Add confectioners' sugar and nuts; mix well. Pour into buttered
9x13-inch dish. Chill until serving time. Cut into squares.
Yield: 60 servings.*

Microwave Peanut Brittle

1 cup raw peanuts
1 cup sugar
$^1/_2$ cup light corn syrup
$^1/_2$ teaspoon salt
1 teaspoon vanilla extract
1 teaspoon butter
1 teaspoon baking soda

Combine peanuts, sugar, corn syrup and salt in glass bowl; mix well.
Microwave on High for 8 minutes, stirring after 4 minutes. Add vanilla and
butter. Microwave for 2 minutes longer. Stir in baking soda until foamy. Pour
onto greased platter. Let stand until cool. Break into pieces.
Yield: 8 servings.

Butterscotch Bars

$^1/_2$ cup butter or margarine
1$^1/_2$ cups graham cracker crumbs
1 cup milk chocolate chips
1 cup butterscotch chips
$^1/_2$ cup shredded coconut
1 cup crisp rice cereal
1 (14-ounce) can sweetened condensed milk

Melt butter in 9x13-inch baking pan; tilt pan to spread evenly. Layer graham
cracker crumbs, chocolate chips, butterscotch chips, coconut, cereal and
condensed milk in pan in order listed; do not mix. Bake at 350 degrees for 15
to 20 minutes or until lightly browned. Cut into bars when cool.
Yield: 32 bars.

Death by Chocolate

1 cup butter, softened
2 cups packed dark brown sugar
2 eggs
1 teaspoon vanilla extract
1$\frac{1}{2}$ cups flour
1 teaspoon baking soda
$\frac{3}{4}$ teaspoon salt
2 cups coarsely crushed cornflakes
2 cups rolled oats
1 cup chopped pecans
Filling

Cream butter and brown sugar in large mixer bowl. Add eggs 1 at a time, beating well after addition. Beat in vanilla. Add sifted flour, baking soda and salt; mix well. Stir in cornflakes, oats and pecans. Press half the mixture into greased 10x15-inch baking pan with floured fingers. Spread Filling evenly over top with spatula, dipping spatula in hot water as necessary. Top with remaining crumb mixture. Bake at 350 degrees for 30 to 35 minutes or until layers pull slightly from sides of pan. Let stand for 5 minutes. Cut into 1$\frac{1}{2}$-inch squares. Cool completely before removing from pan.
Yield: 54 squares.

Filling

2 cups semisweet chocolate chips
2 tablespoons butter
$\frac{3}{4}$ cup sweetened condensed milk
2 teaspoons vanilla extract
$\frac{1}{2}$ teaspoon salt
1 cup finely chopped pecans

Melt chocolate chips and butter in double boiler over hot water; remove from heat. Stir in condensed milk, vanilla and salt; mix well. Stir in pecans.

Carrot Cake Bars

3 eggs ▪ 1¼ cups corn oil
2 cups sugar ▪ 2 cups flour
2 teaspoons baking soda
2 teaspoons ground cinnamon
1 (4-ounce) jar baby food strained carrots
1 (4-ounce) jar baby food applesauce
1 (4-ounce) jar baby food apricots in tapioca
8 ounces cream cheese
½ cup margarine, softened
1 teaspoon vanilla extract
1 small box confectioners' sugar

Beat eggs in mixer bowl. Add oil; mix well. Add next 7 ingredients; stir until thoroughly mixed. Pour into greased 10x20-inch baking pan. Bake at 350 degrees for 35 to 40 minutes; let cool. Beat cream cheese and margarine thoroughly in small mixer bowl. Add vanilla and confectioners' sugar; beat until of spreading consistency. Spread on cooled cake; cut into bars.
Yield: 15 to 20 bars.

Peanut Butter Bars

½ cup butter or margarine ▪ ½ cup sugar
½ cup packed light brown sugar
1 egg ▪ ⅓ cup peanut butter
½ teaspoon baking soda ▪ ¼ teaspoon salt
½ teaspoon vanilla extract
1 cup flour ▪ 1 cup quick-cooking oats
1 cup chocolate chips
½ cup confectioners' sugar
¼ cup peanut butter ▪ ¼ cup milk

Cream first 3 ingredients in mixer bowl. Add next 7 ingredients; mix well. Spread in greased 9x13-inch baking pan. Bake at 350 degrees for 20 to 25 minutes or until layer tests done. Sprinkle chocolate chips on top while warm; spread evenly. Combine remaining ingredients in mixer bowl; blend well. Drizzle on top. Cut into bars.
Yield: 24 bars.

Make your own peanut butter by blending 2 cups peanuts in a blender or food proccessor for 1 minute. Add ¼ cup vegetable oil, 1 tablespoon at a time, processing well after each addition.

Savannah Pecan Bars

1¹/₃ cups flour
¹/₂ cup packed light brown sugar
¹/₃ cup margarine, melted
1 cup chopped pecans
³/₄ cup dark corn syrup
¹/₄ cup packed light brown sugar
¹/₄ cup flour ▪ 2 eggs
1 teaspoon vanilla extract
¹/₂ teaspoon salt

*Combine 1¹/₃ cups flour, ¹/₂ cup brown sugar and margarine in bowl;
mix well. Press into buttered 9x13-inch baking pan. Combine pecans, corn
syrup, ¹/₄ cup brown sugar, ¹/₄ cup flour, eggs, vanilla and salt in bowl;
mix well. Pour over prepared layer. Bake at 350 degrees for 30 to 35 minutes
or until top is set. Let cool. Cut into bars.
Yield: 32 bars.*

Apple Cheddar Cookies

¹/₂ cup butter, softened
¹/₂ cup sugar
1 egg
1 teaspoon vanilla extract
1¹/₂ cups flour
¹/₂ teaspoon baking soda
¹/₂ teaspoon cinnamon
¹/₂ teaspoon salt
1¹/₂ cups shredded Cheddar cheese
1¹/₂ cups chopped peeled apples
¹/₄ cup chopped nuts

*Cream butter and sugar in bowl until light and fluffy. Add egg and vanilla;
mix well. Mix flour, baking soda, cinnamon and salt together. Add to
creamed mixture; mix well. Add cheese, apples and nuts; mix well. Drop by
teaspoonfuls onto ungreased cookie sheet. Bake at 375 degrees for
15 minutes. Cool on wire rack.
Yield: 54 cookies.*

Apricot Jewels

1¼ cups flour ▪ ¼ cup sugar
1½ teaspoons baking powder
¼ teaspoon salt ▪ ½ cup butter or margarine
3 ounces cream cheese ▪ ½ cup shredded coconut
½ cup apricot preserves
1 cup confectioners' sugar
1 tablespoon butter or margarine
¼ cup apricot preserves

*Sift first 4 ingredients together in bowl. Cut in ½ cup butter and
cream cheese. Add coconut and preserves; mixing well. Drop by teaspoonfuls
onto greased cookie sheet. Bake at 350 degrees for 15 to 18 minutes
or until lightly browned; let cool. Combine remaining ingredients in mixer
bowl; blend well. Frost cookies.
Yield: 36 to 48 cookies.*

Brown Sugar Oatmeal Cookies

1½ cups rolled oats ▪ ⅓ cup sour milk
¾ cup margarine, softened
2 cups packed brown sugar
2 eggs ▪ 1 teaspoon vanilla extract
2½ cups pastry flour
1 teaspoon baking powder ▪ 1 teaspoon baking soda
1 teaspoon each cinnamon, nutmeg and cloves
1 teaspoon salt
1 cup chopped dates (optional)
1 cup chopped nuts (optional)

*Toast oats in large shallow baking pan at 350 degrees. Combine with sour
milk in bowl. Let stand for 5 minutes. Cream margarine and brown sugar in
mixer bowl until light. Beat in eggs and vanilla. Add oat mixture and sifted
dry ingredients; mix well. Stir in dates and nuts. Drop by teaspoonfuls
onto greased cookie sheet. Bake at 350 degrees for 10 to 12 minutes or until
golden brown. Cool on wire rack.
Yield: 48 cookies.*

Desserts

Chocolate Chip Cookies with Walnuts

2 cups butter, softened
1¹/₂ cups packed brown sugar
¹/₂ cup sugar ▪ 2 large eggs
1 teaspoon vanilla extract ▪ 4 cups sifted flour
1 tablespoon baking soda ▪ 1 teaspoon salt
1 cup toasted chopped walnuts
1 cup raisins ▪ 2 cups chocolate chips

*Beat butter, brown sugar, sugar, eggs and vanilla in large mixer bowl
for 3 minutes or until smooth. Combine flour, baking soda and salt in medium
bowl; add to butter mixture, mixing thoroughly. Stir in walnuts, raisins
and chocolate chips. Drop by heaping teaspoonfuls 1¹/₂ inches apart onto
greased cookie sheets. Bake at 375 degrees for 10 minutes or until golden
brown. Cool for 1 minute before removing to wire rack to cool completely.
May wrap tightly and freeze if desired.
Yield: 96 cookies.*

German Chocolate Cookies

1 (2-layer) package German chocolate pudding recipe cake mix
¹/₂ cup instant mashed potato flakes
1 teaspoon cream of tartar
1 teaspoon cinnamon ▪ ³/₄ cup melted margarine
3 tablespoons milk ▪ 1 egg
¹/₂ cup chopped nuts ▪ ¹/₄ to ¹/₂ cup sugar
1 cup confectioners' sugar
2 teaspoons baking cocoa
1 tablespoon margarine
2 tablespoons milk

*Combine first 7 ingredients in bowl; mix well. Stir in nuts. Let stand
for 5 minutes. Drop by teaspoonfuls into sugar. Gently toss until coated. Place
2 inches apart on cookie sheet. Bake at 350 degrees for 8 to 10 minutes.
Cool for 5 minutes; remove from cookie sheet. Combine confectioners' sugar,
baking cocoa, 1 tablespoon margarine and 2 tablespoons milk in bowl.
Blend until smooth. Spread on cooled cookies.
Yield: 36 cookies.*

Toast walnuts by first dropping the walnut kernels into boiling water in a saucepan. Boil for 3 minutes and drain. Spread the walnuts in a single layer on a baking sheet. Toast at 350 degrees for 12 to 15 minutes or until golden brown, stirring frequently. Cool before storing in an airtight container in the refrigerator.

Desserts

White Chocolate Chip Cookies

1 cup butter, softened ▪ 1 cup sugar
1 cup packed brown sugar
2 eggs ▪ 1 teaspoon vanilla extract
2 tablespoons baking cocoa
1/2 teaspoon salt ▪ 1 teaspoon baking soda
1 teaspoon baking powder ▪ 2 cups flour
2 1/2 cups quick-cooking oats ▪ 12 ounces white chocolate chips
1 1/2 cups chopped almonds

Cream the butter, sugar and brown sugar in a food processor until smooth. Mix in the eggs and vanilla. Combine the baking cocoa, salt, baking soda and baking powder in a bowl. Add to the food processor and process until moistened. Mix in the flour, scraping down the side of the food processor container as needed. Pulse in the oats. Stir in the chocolate chips and almonds by hand. Shape into 2-inch balls. Place 2 inches apart on ungreased cookie sheets. Bake at 350 degrees for 10 minutes. Remove to a wire rack to cool.
Yield: 48 cookies.

Everyday Cookies

1 cup butter or margarine, softened
1 cup vegetable oil ▪ 1 cup sugar
1 cup packed light brown sugar
2 eggs ▪ 1 teaspoon vanilla extract
3 1/2 cups all-purpose flour
1 teaspoon salt ▪ 1 teaspoon cream of tartar
1 teaspoon baking soda ▪ 1 cup crisp rice cereal
1 cup quick-cooking oats
1 cup unsweetened shredded coconut ▪ 1 cup chopped pecans

Cream butter, oil, sugar and brown sugar in large mixer bowl. Add eggs and vanilla; mix well. Add mixture of flour, salt, cream of tartar and baking soda; mix well. Stir in cereal, oats, coconut and pecans. Drop by teaspoonfuls onto ungreased cookie sheet. Flatten slightly. Bake at 350 degrees on bottom oven rack for 5 minutes. Move to middle oven rack. Bake for 5 minutes longer or until light brown. Remove to wire rack to cool.
Yield: 72 cookies.

Fruit and Pecan Cookies

1 cup margarine, softened
1½ cups sugar ▪ 2 eggs
1½ cups self-rising flour
1 teaspoon baking soda
1 teaspoon salt
1 teaspoon cinnamon
1 cup self-rising flour
2 pounds dates, chopped
½ pound candied cherries, chopped
½ pound candied pineapple, chopped
4 cups chopped pecans

Cream margarine and sugar in large mixer bowl until light and fluffy. Add eggs; mix well. Stir in mixture of 1½ cups flour, baking soda, salt and cinnamon; mix well. Mix 1 cup flour with dates, cherries and pineapple, stirring until fruit is coated. Add to creamed mixture. Stir in pecans. Drop by teaspoonfuls onto ungreased cookie sheet. Bake at 325 to 350 degrees for 10 to 12 minutes or until light brown.
Yield: 120 to 144 cookies.

Orange Slice Cookies

3 eggs
2 cups packed light brown sugar
1 tablespoon cold water
1 teaspoon vanilla extract ▪ 2 cups flour
1 cup chopped orange slice candy
½ cup chopped pitted dates
1 cup chopped pecans

Beat eggs in large mixer bowl until thick and pale yellow. Add brown sugar, water and vanilla; mix well. Sift flour over candy, dates and pecans; toss to coat. Stir candy mixture gently into egg mixture. Chill, covered, for 2 hours. Drop by spoonfuls onto lightly greased cookie sheet. Bake at 350 degrees for 8 minutes or until light brown. Let cookies stand 8 to 12 hours before serving.
Yield: 36 cookies.

Apple Blueberry Crispy Cobbler

1 pint fresh blueberries
2 cups sliced peeled tart apples
1 tablespoon lemon juice
$^{1}/_{2}$ cup packed brown sugar
1 cup flour ▪ $^{3}/_{4}$ cup sugar
1 teaspoon baking powder
$^{3}/_{4}$ teaspoon salt ▪ 1 egg, lightly beaten
$^{1}/_{3}$ cup butter, melted, cooled
$^{1}/_{2}$ teaspoon cinnamon

Combine blueberries and apples in buttered 8x8-inch baking dish.
Sprinkle with lemon juice and brown sugar. Combine flour, sugar, baking
powder and salt in medium bowl. Add egg and mix well. Sprinkle over
fruit and drizzle with melted butter. Sprinkle with cinnamon. Bake at 350
degrees for 35 to 40 minutes or until fruit is bubbling and topping is brown.
Serve warm with ice cream or whipped cream.
Yield: 6 servings.

Marble-Top Apricot Pie

$^{1}/_{2}$ cup sugar ▪ $^{1}/_{3}$ cup flour
$^{1}/_{4}$ teaspoon salt ▪ $^{3}/_{4}$ cup milk
$1^{1}/_{4}$ cups puréed apricots
2 egg yolks, beaten
2 tablespoons butter or margarine
Juice of 1 lemon ▪ 1 baked (9-inch) pie shell
8 ounces whipped topping
$^{1}/_{4}$ square unsweetened chocolate

Combine sugar, flour, salt and milk in double boiler. Cook over medium
heat until thickened, stirring constantly. Remove from heat. Add apricots and
egg yolks gradually, stirring constantly. Cook for 5 to 10 minutes longer,
stirring frequently. Mix in butter and lemon juice. Cool. Pour into pie shell.
Spread with whipped topping. Place chocolate in small glass container.
Microwave on High for 2 minutes or until melted. Cool. Pour over whipped
topping, spreading to give marble appearance.
Yield: 8 servings.

White Chocolate Raspberry Pie

12 ounces white chocolate
$^{1}/_{2}$ cup whipping cream
$^{1}/_{4}$ cup butter or margarine
2 teaspoons light corn syrup
1 pint fresh raspberries
1 baked (10-inch) tart shell
1 (10-ounce) package frozen raspberries in heavy syrup, thawed

Cut chocolate into small pieces. Microwave in glass bowl until softened. Combine whipping cream, butter and corn syrup in saucepan. Bring to a boil, stirring frequently. Pour over chocolate; stir until blended and smooth. Stir in fresh raspberries. Spoon into tart shell. Chill in the refrigerator until firm. Serve with thawed raspberries.
Yield: 12 servings.

Caramel Pies

1 cup chopped pecans
1 (7-ounce) can flaked coconut
2 tablespoons melted margarine
1 (14-ounce) can sweetened condensed milk
8 ounces cream cheese, softened
16 ounces whipped topping
1 (20-ounce) jar caramel ice cream topping
2 unbaked (10-inch) deep-dish pie shells

Combine pecans, coconut and margarine in bowl; mix well. Spread on baking sheet. Toast in moderate oven until light brown, stirring occasionally. Beat condensed milk and cream cheese in mixer bowl until smooth. Fold in whipped topping. Layer cream cheese mixture, ice cream topping and pecan mixture $^{1}/_{2}$ at a time in each pie shell. Chill until serving time.
Yield: 12 servings.

Ice Cream Pie with Meringue Crust

1 egg white ▪ ¹/₄ cup sugar
1¹/₂ cups chopped pecans
1 quart vanilla ice cream, softened
8 pecan halves ▪ Caramel Raisin Sauce

*Beat egg white at high speed in mixer bowl until soft peaks form. Add sugar 1
tablespoon at a time, beating until stiff peaks form and sugar dissolves.
Fold in chopped pecans. Spread mixture over bottom and up side of 9-inch pie
plate. Bake at 400 degrees for 12 minutes or until brown. Cool completely.
Spread ice cream evenly over crust. Cover and freeze until ice cream is firm.
Place pecan halves over ice cream. Top with Caramel Raisin Sauce.
Yield: 8 servings.*

Caramel Raisin Sauce

3 tablespoons butter
1 cup packed light brown sugar ▪ ¹/₂ cup whipping cream
¹/₂ cup golden raisins ▪ 1 teaspoon vanilla extract

*Melt butter in saucepan. Add brown sugar and cream. Cook over low heat until
sugar dissolves, stirring constantly. Add raisins and vanilla; mix well.
Yield: 1¹/₂ cups.*

Lemon Chess Pie

¹/₄ cup butter, softened
1¹/₂ cups sugar ▪ 1 tablespoon flour
3 eggs, lightly beaten
Juice and grated peel of 1 lemon
2 tablespoons milk ▪ 1 teaspoon vanilla extract
¹/₈ teaspoon salt ▪ 1 unbaked (9-inch) pie shell

*Cream butter and sugar in mixer bowl until light and fluffy. Add flour;
mix well. Stir in eggs, lemon juice, lemon peel, milk, vanilla and salt. Spoon
into pie shell. Bake at 325 degrees for 45 to 50 minutes or just until set.
Do not overbake, as pie may separate into layers.
Yield: 8 servings.*

Lime Pie

8 ounces cream cheese, softened
1 (14-ounce) can sweetened condensed milk
1 (6-ounce) can frozen limeade concentrate, thawed
1 or 2 drops of green food coloring
8 ounces whipped topping
1 baked (9-inch) pie shell

*Beat cream cheese in mixer bowl until light and fluffy. Blend in
condensed milk and limeade concentrate. Stir in food coloring. Fold in whipped
topping. Spoon into pie shell. Chill for 4 to 6 hours or until firm.
May use graham cracker pie shell.
Yield: 6 servings.*

Fresh Peach Pie

5 fresh peaches, peeled, thinly sliced
5 slices bread, cubed
Nutmeg to taste
$\frac{1}{2}$ cup melted margarine
$1\frac{1}{4}$ cups sugar
2 tablespoons flour
1 egg
$\frac{1}{2}$ teaspoon vanilla extract

*Layer peaches and bread cubes in pie plate. Sprinkle with nutmeg.
Combine margarine, sugar, flour, egg and vanilla in bowl; mix well. Pour over
layers. Bake at 350 degrees for 25 to 30 minutes or until brown.
Yield: 8 servings.*

Nuts

Cilantro Pesto

1/2 bunch spinach
1/2 bunch fresh cilantro
3 cloves of garlic, minced
1/3 cup grated Parmesan cheese
1/4 cup walnuts
1/3 cup olive oil

Rinse spinach; pat dry with paper towels. Remove stems; chop coarsely. Combine spinach, cilantro, garlic, cheese and walnuts in food processor container; process until finely chopped. Add olive oil in fine stream, processing constantly at high speed until smooth. Toss with warm pasta or serve as spread on French bread. May substitute basil or tarragon for cilantro.
Yield: 2 cups.

Four-Cheese Pâté

24 ounces cream cheese, softened
2 tablespoons milk
2 tablespoons sour cream
3/4 cup chopped pecans
4 ounces Camembert cheese with rind, at room temperature
1 cup shredded Swiss cheese, at room temperature
4 ounces bleu cheese, crumbled, at room temperature
1/2 cup pecan halves
2 red apples, cut into wedges
2 green apples, cut into wedges

Line 9-inch pie plate with plastic wrap. Beat 8 ounces of cream cheese with milk and sour cream in mixer bowl until smooth. Spread evenly in prepared pie plate. Sprinkle with chopped pecans. Beat remaining 16 ounces cream cheese, Camembert cheese, Swiss cheese and bleu cheese in mixer bowl until blended. Spread evenly over chopped pecans. Chill, covered with plastic wrap, for up to 1 week. Invert onto platter just before serving; discard plastic wrap. Arrange pecan halves over top; surround pâté with apple wedges.
Yield: 4 1/2 cups.

California produces 70 percent of the world's supply of walnuts and 99 percent of all the walnuts grown commercially in this country. It exports walnuts to more than 100 other countries.

Nuts

Hot Pecan Spread

1/2 cup chopped pecans
1 tablespoon butter
8 ounces cream cheese, softened
1/3 cup sour cream
1/2 cup finely chopped green bell pepper
2 green onions with tops, minced
1 (2-ounce) jar dried beef, chopped
1 to 2 teaspoons minced garlic
3 to 4 dashes of onion salt
Freshly ground pepper to taste

Sauté pecans in butter in skillet for 2 minutes or until brown and crisp. Combine cream cheese and sour cream in bowl; mix well. Stir in green pepper, green onions, dried beef, garlic, onion salt and pepper. Spoon into baking dish; sprinkle with pecans. Bake at 350 degrees for 15 to 20 minutes. Serve with melba toast rounds or assorted party crackers.
Yield: 24 servings.

Peanut Buttered Popcorn

3 quarts popped popcorn
1 1/2 cups unblanched whole almonds
1 cup sugar
1/2 cup honey
1/2 cup light corn syrup
1 cup peanut butter
1 teaspoon vanilla extract

Combine popcorn and almonds in large baking pan. Place in 250-degree oven to keep warm. Butter inside of heavy 1 1/2-quart saucepan. Add sugar, honey and corn syrup; bring to a boil. Boil for 2 minutes, stirring constantly. Remove from heat; stir in peanut butter and vanilla. Pour over popcorn mixture, stirring to coat. Let cool. Break into bite-size pieces. May substitute dry-roasted peanuts or mixed nuts for almonds if desired.
Yield: 24 servings.

Peanut Soup

1 medium onion, minced ▪ 2 ribs celery, minced
¹/₄ cup butter ▪ 2 tablespoons flour
1 cup crunchy peanut butter
4 cups chicken broth ▪ 1 tablespoon lemon juice
Salt and pepper to taste

*Sauté onion and celery in butter in skillet. Sprinkle with flour; mix well.
Spoon into top of double boiler over boiling water. Add peanut butter, stirring
until melted. Add chicken broth, lemon juice, salt and pepper. Cook over
boiling water until heated through. Garnish individual servings with ground
peanuts and chopped parsley.
Yield: 7 servings.*

Brown Rice Salad

1 cup brown rice
3 green scallions, finely chopped
1 red bell pepper, chopped ▪ ¹/₄ cup raisins
¹/₄ cup roasted cashews, chopped
2 tablespoons chopped parsley
6 tablespoons Soy Sauce Dressing

*Cook rice in boiling water to cover in saucepan for 40 to 45 minutes or
until tender. Rinse; drain well. Let cool. Combine rice, scallions, red pepper,
raisins, cashews and parsley in salad bowl. Add 6 tablespoons Soy
Sauce Dressing; toss to coat.
Yield: 6 servings.*

Soy Sauce Dressing

³/₄ cup olive oil ▪ ¹/₄ cup light soy sauce
2 tablespoons lemon juice ▪ 1 clove of garlic, crushed
1 (¹/₂-inch) piece gingerroot, finely chopped

*Combine olive oil, soy sauce, lemon juice, garlic, and gingerroot
in jar with tightfitting lid. Shake well.
Yield: 1¹/₈ cups.*

Strawberry and Kiwi Spinach Salad

5 cups fresh spinach leaves
8 to 10 firm ripe strawberries, sliced
1 kiwifruit, peeled, sliced
¼ cup slivered almonds
½ cup crumbled feta cheese
4 to 8 thinly sliced red onion rings
Poppy seed salad dressing

Rinse spinach leaves, discarding stems; pat dry. Combine spinach, strawberries and kiwifruit in large salad bowl. Add almonds, feta cheese and onion rings; toss lightly. Add poppy seed dressing; toss lightly. Yield: 2 to 4 servings.

Stir-Fried Orange Beef

1 pound lean beef (round or sirloin)
1 tablespoon soy sauce
2 tablespoons honey
2 tablespoons cornstarch
1 teaspoon grated fresh gingerroot
⅛ teaspoon dried red pepper flakes
Freshly ground black pepper to taste
Zest of 1 whole orange, sliced into julienne strips
¾ cup shelled pistachios
2 scallions, sliced diagonally
6 tablespoons peanut oil

Slice beef thinly across the grain. Combine soy sauce, honey, cornstarch, gingerroot and red and black pepper in bowl. Stir in beef. Stir-fry orange zest, pistachios and scallions in oil in wok for 1 minute. Remove with slotted spoon. Stir-fry beef mixture in hot oil for 2 to 3 minutes. Return pistachio mixture to wok. Stir-fry for 30 seconds. Arrange on serving platter. Serve with rice. Yield: 4 to 6 servings.

Ground Beef Stroganoff

¹/₃ cup chopped onion
¹/₄ cup margarine
1 pound ground beef
2 tablespoons flour
1 teaspoon salt
1 teaspoon pepper
¹/₄ teaspoon paprika
1 (8-ounce) can sliced mushrooms, drained
1 (8-ounce) can sliced water chestnuts, drained
1 (10-ounce) can cream of chicken soup
1 cup sour cream
8 ounces noodles, cooked

Sauté onion in margarine in large skillet. Combine ground beef, flour and seasonings in large bowl; add to onion. Cook until ground beef loses red color, stirring until crumbly; drain. Add mushrooms, water chestnuts and soup; mix well. Cook over low heat for 5 minutes. Stir in sour cream; remove from heat. Serve over noodles.
Yield: 4 to 6 servings.

Chutney Lamb Chops

12 lamb chops
Salt and pepper to taste
3 tablespoons olive oil
2 tablespoons Dijon mustard
2 tablespoons white grape juice
¹/₂ cup mango chutney, puréed
²/₃ cup peanuts, chopped

Sprinkle chops with salt and pepper. Sauté chops in oil over high heat until golden brown and rare inside. Transfer chops to greased baking dish. Mix mustard and grape juice until smooth. Brush mustard mixture on chops and sprinkle with chutney and peanuts. Bake at 400 degrees for 5 minutes.
Yield: 6 servings.

Nuts

Grilled Butterflied Pork Chops

2 tablespoons butter ▪ 4 green onions, chopped
¹/₂ cup sliced fresh mushrooms ▪ 2 cloves of garlic, crushed
¹/₂ teaspoon ginger powder ▪ 2 tablespoons apple juice
1¹/₂ cups imitation crab meat ▪ ¹/₂ cup shredded Swiss cheese
¹/₂ cup shredded sharp Cheddar cheese
¹/₄ cup whole cashews ▪ 4 (1-inch-thick) butterflied pork chops

*Melt butter in large skillet. Add next 5 ingredients. Cook until green onions are
tender. Add crab meat; mix well. Add cheeses. Cook over low heat until cheese
is melted, stirring constantly. Remove from heat. Add cashews, stirring gently.
Stuff chops with filling. Place on heated grill. Grill until cooked through.
Yield: 4 servings.*

Microwave Pork Hawaiian

1 (20-ounce) can juice-pack pineapple chunks
¹/₃ cup wine vinegar ▪ ¹/₄ cup soy sauce
1 tablespoon cornstarch ▪ 3 cups cubed cooked pork
¹/₃ cup packed brown sugar
2 tablespoons cornstarch ▪ ¹/₂ teaspoon ginger
¹/₄ teaspoon garlic powder ▪ ¹/₄ cup soy sauce
2 tablespoons catsup ▪ 1 onion, cut into chunks
1 green bell pepper, cut into chunks
1 (8-ounce) can water chestnuts, drained
1 (3-ounce) jar sliced mushrooms, drained ▪ 4 to 6 cups cooked rice

*Drain pineapple, reserving juice. Combine reserved juice with enough water to
measure 1 cup. Add vinegar and ¹/₄ cup soy sauce; mix well. Stir in 1
tablespoon cornstarch. Place pork in microwave-safe glass dish. Pour mixture
of brown sugar, 2 tablespoons cornstarch, ginger, garlic powder, ¹/₄ cup soy
sauce and catsup over pork. Microwave on High for 3 minutes. Add onion and
green pepper; mix well. Microwave on High for 4 minutes. Pour pineapple
juice mixture over pork. Microwave on High for 6 minutes or until vegetables
are tender-crisp and pork is cooked through, stirring twice. Add pineapple,
water chestnuts and mushrooms; mix well. Microwave on High for 2 to 3
minutes or until heated through. Serve over hot rice.
Yield: 8 servings.*

Chicken Macadamia

3 whole chicken breasts, boned
Salt to taste
2 eggs
1/2 cup flour
1/4 cup cornstarch
1/2 cup cold water
1 tablespoon minced fresh ginger
1 medium onion, grated
1/4 teaspoon pepper
2 tablespoons corn oil
2 tablespoons soy sauce
2 tablespoons brandy
Vegetable oil for deep-frying
1 tablespoon cornstarch
1/2 cup packed light brown sugar
1/3 cup vinegar
6 tablespoons pineapple juice
2 tablespoons soy sauce
1/4 cup chopped green bell pepper
1 small can macadamia nuts, chopped
Shredded coconut

Rinse chicken and pat dry. Sprinkle chicken lightly with salt. Let stand for 30 minutes. Combine eggs, flour, cornstarch, cold water, ginger, onion, pepper, corn oil and 2 tablespoons soy sauce in bowl; beat until smooth. Marinate chicken in batter for 20 minutes. Deep-fry in hot oil until golden brown and cooked through; drain. Keep warm in oven. Mix 1 tablespoon cornstarch, brown sugar, vinegar, pineapple juice and 2 tablespoons soy sauce in saucepan. Cook until thickened, stirring constantly. Add additional pineapple juice if necessary to make of desired consistency. Stir in green pepper. Pour over chicken. Top with macadamia nuts; sprinkle with coconut. Serve immediately. Yield: 6 servings.

Honey Pecan Chicken

4 boneless skinless chicken breasts
1/2 cup buttermilk ▪ 2 cups flour
1/8 teaspoon cayenne pepper
1/2 teaspoon salt
1/4 teaspoon black pepper
1/4 teaspoon garlic powder
Vegetable oil
1/4 cup butter or margarine
1/4 cup honey ▪ 1/4 cup roasted pecans

Rinse chicken and pat dry. Pound chicken until flattened; cut into halves. Soak in buttermilk in bowl for 2 hours. Combine flour and seasonings in bowl. Coat chicken with flour mixture. Let stand for 20 minutes; coat again. Pour oil to 1-inch depth in skillet. Fry chicken until golden brown and cooked through, turning halfway through cooking time. Melt butter and honey in saucepan. Stir in pecans. Place chicken in serving dish. Pour honey pecan sauce over top. Serve.
Yield: 4 servings.

Almond Chicken

3 chicken breast fillets
3 tablespoons peanut oil
2 (5-ounce) cans bamboo shoots, drained, sliced
2 cups diagonally sliced celery
1/2 cup blanched slivered almonds
2 (5-ounce) cans water chestnuts, drained, sliced
2 tablespoons soy sauce ▪ 3 cups chicken broth
3 tablespoons cornstarch
1/2 cup water

Cut chicken into thin slices; rinse and pat dry. Stir-fry in hot oil in wok over high heat until brown. Add bamboo shoots, celery, almonds, water chestnuts, soy sauce and chicken broth; mix well. Simmer, covered, for 5 minutes. Stir in mixture of cornstarch and water. Cook until thickened, stirring constantly. Serve with rice.
Yield: 4 servings.

Almonds are a good source of vegetable protein and one of the best sources of Vitamin E. High in riboflavin, they also contain significant amounts of copper, iron, magnesium, phosphorus, calcium, zinc, niacin, thiamin, and folacin.

Chicken Pecan Fettuccini

3/4 cup butter
1 pound skinned and boned chicken breasts, cut into 3/4-inch pieces
3 cups sliced mushrooms ▪ 1 cup sliced green onions
1/2 teaspoon salt ▪ 1/2 teaspoon pepper
1/2 teaspoon garlic powder ▪ 10 ounces fettuccini
1 egg yolk ▪ 2/3 cup half-and-half, at room temperature
2 tablespoons chopped fresh parsley
1/2 cup grated Parmesan cheese
1 cup pecans, toasted and chopped

Melt 1/4 cup of butter in skillet. Rinse chicken and pat dry. Add chicken to skillet and sauté until light brown. Remove chicken from skillet. Sauté mushrooms and green onions in drippings in skillet. Return chicken to skillet and simmer for 15 minutes or until cooked through. Add 1/4 teaspoon of salt, 1/4 teaspoon of pepper and 1/4 teaspoon of garlic powder. Cook fettuccini using package directions; drain. Melt remaining butter and combine with egg yolk, half-and-half, parsley and remaining salt, pepper and garlic powder. Stir mixture into hot fettuccini. Add Parmesan cheese and chicken mixture and toss. Sprinkle with pecans.
Yield: 4 servings.

Oriental Cashew Chicken

2 skinless boneless chicken breasts, sliced
2 cloves of garlic, minced ▪ 2 tablespoons soy sauce
2 tablespoons cornstarch ▪ 1 tablespoon water
1/4 teaspoon ginger ▪ 2 tablespoons vegetable oil
1 medium green bell pepper, cut into 1-inch squares
1/2 cup cashews

Rinse chicken and pat dry. Combine chicken and next 5 ingredients in medium bowl; mix well. Chill for 15 minutes. Microwave oil in 7x11-inch glass dish on High for 2 1/2 minutes. Add chicken mixture. Microwave on High for 5 minutes, stirring twice. Add green pepper and cashews. Cover loosely with plastic wrap. Microwave on High for 5 minutes. Let stand, covered, for 3 minutes. Stir and serve.
Yield: 4 servings.

Glazed Cornish Hens

8 Cornish game hens
1 recipe Pecan Rice Stuffing
1/4 cup margarine, softened
2 cups apple juice
1 to 3 teaspoons honey
1 to 3 teaspoons Dijon mustard

Rinse hens inside and out; pat dry. Stuff with Pecan Rice Stuffing; secure with skewers. Place in shallow roasting pan. Rub with margarine. Roast at 375 degrees for 45 minutes or until drumstick moves easily, basting occasionally with pan juices. Bring apple juice to a boil in saucepan. Boil for 20 minutes or until reduced to 1 cup. Place hens on serving plate. Stir pan juices into apple juice. Whisk in honey and mustard. Spoon over hens.
Yield: 8 servings.

Pecan Rice Stuffing

2 tablespoons butter
1 teaspoon curry powder
2 teaspoons cumin
1 1/2 cups uncooked long grain rice
4 cups chicken bouillon
3 green onions with tops, thinly sliced
1/2 cup golden raisins
1/2 cup coarsely chopped pecans

Heat butter, curry powder and cumin in large heavy saucepan. Add rice. Cook over medium heat, stirring until coated. Add bouillon. Bring to a boil, stirring frequently; reduce heat. Simmer, covered, for 45 minutes or until most of liquid is absorbed. Remove from heat. Stir in green onions, raisins and pecans.
Yield: 6 cups.

Sautéed Turkey with Pecans

1 pound turkey breast slices
2 cloves of garlic, chopped
1 to 2 tablespoons olive oil
1 teaspoon cracked peppercorns
1/3 cup apple juice
2 tablespoons whipping cream
2 pears, sliced 1/4 inch thick
1/4 to 1/2 cup pecan halves, toasted
Cooked rice

Rinse turkey and pat dry. Sauté turkey and garlic in hot oil in skillet for 1 to 2 minutes or until brown and cooked through; reduce heat. Stir in peppercorns, apple juice, cream and pears. Cook for 1 to 2 minutes or until heated through. Arrange on serving platter. Top with toasted pecans. Serve over rice. Yield: 4 servings.

Catfish Parmesan

1/3 cup sliced almonds
2/3 cup Parmesan cheese
1/4 cup flour
1/2 teaspoon salt
1/4 teaspoon pepper
1 teaspoon paprika
1 egg, beaten
1/4 cup milk
5 or 6 small catfish fillets
1/4 cup melted margarine

Place almonds in shallow baking pan. Roast at 400 degrees for 4 to 6 minutes or until light brown. Cool. Combine Parmesan cheese, flour, salt, pepper and paprika in shallow bowl; mix well. Beat egg with milk in bowl. Dip catfish in egg mixture; dredge in cheese mixture. Arrange in lightly greased 9x13-inch baking dish. Drizzle with margarine; sprinkle with almonds. Reduce oven temperature to 350 degrees. Bake for 35 minutes or until catfish flakes easily. Yield: 5 to 6 servings.

Nuts

Trout with Grapes and Almonds

1 cup flour ▪ Salt and pepper to taste
12 ounces trout, boned and butterflied
1/2 cup half-and-half ▪ 1/4 cup olive oil
6 tablespoons butter or margarine
1/3 cup lemon juice ▪ 1 cup fresh white grapes
1/2 cup sliced almonds

Combine flour with salt and pepper. Dip trout in half-and-half and dredge with seasoned flour. Sauté trout in oil in skillet for 5 to 6 minutes or until golden brown on both sides. Drain trout on paper towels. Melt butter in skillet until light brown. Stir in lemon juice, grapes and almonds. Place trout on warm plates and pour mixture over trout. Garnish with lemon wedges and parsley. Yield: 2 servings.

Spicy Shrimp with Walnuts

1 cup walnut halves
1/2 cup soy sauce ▪ 1/4 cup vegetable oil
1/2 cup chicken broth ▪ 2 tablespoons sesame oil
1 1/2 tablespoons sugar
8 dried chile peppers, chopped
2 tablespoons minced garlic
2 tablespoons fresh minced ginger
3 pounds large fresh shrimp, peeled
2 tablespoons peanut oil
1 1/2 bunches green onions, sliced into 1 1/2-inch pieces

Place walnuts on baking sheet. Toast in oven at 250 degrees for 15 minutes. Combine soy sauce, vegetable oil, chicken broth, sesame oil, sugar, chile peppers, garlic and ginger in large bowl; mix well. Add shrimp, stirring to coat with marinade. Marinate in refrigerator for 30 minutes to 1 1/2 hours. Drain, reserving marinade. Stir-fry shrimp in hot peanut oil in wok for 3 to 4 minutes or until shrimp turn pink. Remove to warm platter. Pour reserved marinade and toasted walnuts into wok. Bring to a boil. Cook until mixture becomes syrupy, stirring constantly. Add shrimp and green onions, tossing to coat. Serve with cooked rice. Yield: 6 servings.

Broccoli and Walnut Casserole

3 pounds fresh broccoli, or 3 (10-ounce) packages frozen broccoli
1/4 cup flour
1 1/2 tablespoons instant chicken bouillon
1/2 cup melted butter
2 cups milk
6 tablespoons butter
2/3 cup hot water
2 cups stuffing mix
2/3 cup chopped walnuts

Cook broccoli just until tender using package directions; drain. Arrange in buttered 9x13-inch baking dish. Stir flour and bouillon into 1/2 cup melted butter in saucepan. Add milk. Cook until thickened, stirring constantly. Spoon over broccoli. Melt 6 tablespoons butter in hot water in bowl. Stir in stuffing mix. Add chopped walnuts; mix well. Spread over casserole. Bake at 350 degrees for 30 minutes.
Yield: 10 servings.

One ounce or 1/4 cup of shelled walnuts contains 192 calories, 5 grams of protein, and 19 grams of fat.

Cranberry and Apple Casserole

4 or 5 medium apples, unpeeled, chopped
1 pound cranberries
2 cups rolled oats
2 cups sugar
3/4 cup packed brown sugar
1/3 cup flour
1/2 cup chopped pecans
3/4 cup melted margarine

Layer apples and cranberries in greased 9x13-inch baking dish. Sprinkle with mixture of oats and sugar. Combine brown sugar, flour, pecans and melted margarine in bowl; mix well. Spread over top. Bake at 350 degrees for 45 to 60 minutes or until fruit is tender and casserole is brown.
Yield: 15 servings.

Nuts

Almond Green Beans

8 slices bacon ▪ ¹/₂ cup sugar
¹/₄ cup red wine vinegar
1 small package sliced almonds
2 (16-ounce) cans green beans, drained
1 bunch green onions, chopped

Fry bacon in skillet until crisp; remove and crumble bacon, reserving drippings in skillet. Stir in sugar, wine vinegar and almonds. Bring to a boil. Pour over beans and green onions in baking dish; top with bacon. Bake at 350 degrees for 20 minutes.
Yield: 10 servings.

Baked Stuffed Onions

6 medium Vidalia or other sweet onions
1 clove of garlic, pressed ▪ ¹/₂ teaspoon vegetable oil
1 bunch spinach, coarsely chopped
¹/₂ teaspoon salt ▪ ¹/₄ cup golden raisins, plumped
¹/₂ cup plain yogurt ▪ ¹/₄ cup toasted pine nuts
1 tablespoon grated orange zest
¹/₈ teaspoon nutmeg
3 tablespoons fresh bread crumbs

Trim thin slice from root ends of onions to level. Cut ¹/₂-inch slice from tops of onions and reserve. Hollow out onions with melon baller, leaving ¹/₂-inch shells; reserve centers. Place onion shells on rack in steamer over 1 inch boiling water. Steam, covered, for 10 to 15 minutes or until onions appear tender when pierced with point of knife; invert to drain. Chop reserved onion slices and centers. Sauté chopped onion and garlic in oil in skillet over medium heat until brown. Add spinach. Cook until spinach is wilted. Add salt. Cook until moisture has evaporated, stirring occasionally. Cool in bowl. Add raisins, yogurt, pine nuts, orange zest and nutmeg; mix well. Spoon spinach mixture into drained onion shells; spread any remaining stuffing mixture in baking dish. Place onions in prepared dish; sprinkle with bread crumbs. Bake at 350 degrees for 20 to 25 minutes Broil just until golden brown. Serve with additional stuffing mixture.
Yield: 6 servings.

Nuts

Sweet Potatoes with Topping

1 (29-ounce) can sweet potatoes
3 tablespoons butter
1/4 cup packed brown sugar
1/4 teaspoon salt ▪ Whipping cream
2/3 cup packed brown sugar
1 tablespoon whipping cream
1/2 cup chopped pecans
3 tablespoons butter
1/2 teaspoon ground cinnamon
1/4 teaspoon ground nutmeg
1/8 teaspoon salt
1/4 teaspoon ground ginger
1/8 teaspoon ground cloves

*Heat undrained sweet potatoes in saucepan until heated through; drain. Combine with 3 tablespoons butter, 1/4 cup brown sugar and 1/4 teaspoon salt in bowl. Mash well, adding enough whipping cream to make of desired consistency. Spoon into buttered 2-quart baking dish. Combine 2/3 cup brown sugar, 1 tablespoon whipping cream, pecans, 3 tablespoons butter, cinnamon, nutmeg, 1/8 teaspoon salt, ginger and cloves in small saucepan. Cook over medium heat until butter melts, stirring until smooth. Spread over sweet potatoes. Bake at 350 degrees for 10 to 15 minutes or until bubbly.
Yield: 6 to 8 servings.*

Spinach Delight

2 (10-ounce) packages frozen spinach
1 (5-ounce) can sliced water chestnuts
4 slices crisp-fried bacon, crumbled
1 (10-ounce) can Cheddar cheese soup
1 (3-ounce) can French-fried onions

*Cook spinach using package directions; drain and cut into pieces with scissors. Place in 7x10-inch baking dish. Top with water chestnuts and bacon. Spread soup over top. Top with onions. Bake at 350 degrees for 20 to 25 minutes.
Yield: 8 to 10 servings.*

Nuts

Pecan Crisp Squash

2 acorn squash
2/3 cup butter cracker crumbs
1/3 cup coarsely chopped pecans
1/3 cup melted margarine
3 tablespoons brown sugar
1/2 teaspoon salt
1/4 teaspoon nutmeg

Microwave whole squash on High for 2 minutes. Cut squash into halves; remove seeds. Place cut side down on 8x12-inch microwave-safe baking dish. Cover with plastic wrap, leaving corners open to vent. Microwave on High for 6 minutes, turning twice. Combine cracker crumbs, pecans, margarine, brown sugar, salt and nutmeg in small bowl; mix well. Spoon mixture into squash. Microwave, covered, on High for 6 to 8 minutes or until squash is tender, turning once. Remove plastic wrap. Let stand for 5 minutes before serving.
Yield: 4 servings.

Buy in-shell pecans that are clean, not broken, and do not rattle when shaken. Shelled pecans should be crisp and plump.

Banana Hazelnut Bread

1/4 cup chopped hazelnuts
1/4 cup dates
2 1/4 cups self-rising flour
1/3 cup packed light brown sugar
1 cup mashed bananas
1/2 cup buttermilk
1/4 cup skim milk powder
2 tablespoons light corn syrup
2 egg whites

Combine hazelnuts, dates, flour and brown sugar in large bowl. Stir in bananas. Add buttermilk, milk powder, corn syrup and egg whites gradually, mixing well after each addition. Pour into lightly greased 5x9-inch loaf pan. Bake at 350 degrees for 45 minutes or until wooden pick inserted in center comes out clean.
Yield: 12 servings.

Nuts

Macadamia Nut Loaves

3 cups flour ▪ ¹/₄ teaspoon salt
¹/₂ teaspoon baking powder
1 cup butter or margarine, softened
¹/₂ cup shortening ▪ 3 cups sugar
1 teaspoon lemon extract ▪ 1 teaspoon coconut extract
1 teaspoon vanilla extract ▪ 1 teaspoon almond extract ▪ 5 eggs
1 cup milk ▪ 1 (20-ounce) can crushed pineapple, drained
5 ounces macadamia nuts ▪ 1 cup shredded coconut

Sift flour, salt and baking powder in bowl, reserving ¹/₂ cup. Cream butter, shortening and sugar in mixer bowl until light. Add flavorings; mix well. Beat in eggs 1 at a time. Add dry ingredients alternately with milk to creamed mixture, mixing well after each addition. Combine reserved ¹/₂ cup flour mixture with pineapple, macadamia nuts and coconut in medium bowl; toss until coated. Stir into batter. Spoon into 3 greased and floured 5x9-inch loaf pans. Bake at 325 degrees for 1 hour.
Yield: 3 loaves.

Pear Nut Bread

1 (16-ounce) can Bartlett pear halves
¹/₄ cup vegetable oil ▪ 1 egg, beaten
2 teaspoons grated orange peel ▪ 2¹/₂ cups flour ▪ ¹/₂ cup sugar
1 tablespoon baking powder ▪ 1 teaspoon salt
¹/₈ teaspoon nutmeg ▪ ¹/₂ cup chopped walnuts
1 cup confectioners' sugar ▪ 1 to 2 tablespoons orange juice

Drain pears, reserving syrup. Reserve 1 pear half; cut into 6 slices. Process remaining pears in blender or food processor until puréed. Combine puréed pears with enough reserved syrup to measure 1 cup. Stir in oil, egg and orange peel. Mix next 5 ingredients in bowl. Stir in pear mixture. Fold in walnuts. Spoon into greased loaf pan. Arrange reserved pear slices crosswise over batter. Bake at 350 degrees for 50 to 55 minutes or until loaf tests done. Cool in pan for 5 minutes. Invert onto wire rack. Drizzle warm bread with mixture of confectioners' sugar and orange juice. Cool completely. Wrap in foil. Let stand overnight before slicing.
Yield: 12 servings.

Pecan Bread

2½ cups sifted flour
1 cup sugar
1 teaspoon salt
2 teaspoons baking powder
1 cup instant nonfat dry milk
1 cup water
2 eggs, beaten
1 cup chopped pecans

Sift first 5 ingredients together in bowl. Stir water into eggs in bowl. Add eggs and pecans to dry ingredients, mixing just until blended. Spoon batter into greased 5x9-inch loaf pan. Bake at 350 degrees for 50 to 60 minutes. Let cool in pan for 10 minutes. Invert onto rack; remove paper from bottom. Yield: 12 to 15 servings.

Peanut Butter Bran Muffins

1 cup flour
⅓ cup packed light brown sugar
2 teaspoons baking powder
½ teaspoon salt
1 cup bran cereal
1 cup raisins
1 egg, beaten
1 cup milk
½ cup chunky peanut butter
3 tablespoons vegetable oil

Combine flour, brown sugar, baking powder and salt in bowl. Add bran cereal and raisins; mix well. Blend egg with milk in small bowl. Add peanut butter and oil; mix well. Add to dry ingredients; mix just until moistened. Fill greased muffin cups ⅔ full. Bake at 400 degrees for 15 minutes or until muffins test done. Remove to wire rack to cool. Yield: 12 servings.

Peanuts are high in niacin and are important also for other B Vitamins. The high fat content of peanuts makes them a good source of energy.

Coconut Pumpkin Praline Muffins

2 cups flour ▪ 3/4 cup packed light brown sugar
1/2 cup shredded coconut ▪ 1/2 cup chopped pecans
2 1/4 teaspoons pumpkin pie spice
2 teaspoons baking powder ▪ 1 egg
1 cup solid-pack pumpkin
1/2 cup milk ▪ 1/3 cup vegetable oil
1/2 cup packed light brown sugar
1/2 cup shredded coconut
1/2 cup chopped pecans ▪ 3 tablespoons milk

Combine flour, 3/4 cup brown sugar, 1/2 cup coconut, 1/2 cup pecans, pumpkin pie spice and baking powder in large bowl; mix well. Combine egg, pumpkin, 1/2 cup milk and oil in medium bowl; mix until blended. Stir into flour mixture. Spoon into greased or paper-lined medium muffin cups, filling 3/4 full. Combine 1/2 cup brown sugar, 1/2 cup coconut, 1/2 cup pecans and 3 tablespoons milk in small bowl; mix well. Sprinkle over batter. Bake at 400 degrees for 18 to 20 minutes or until wooden pick inserted in center comes out clean. Cool in pan for 15 minutes. Remove to wire rack to cool completely.
Yield: 12 servings.

Fudge Pudding Cake

3/4 cup sugar ▪ 1 tablespoon butter or margarine, softened
1/2 cup milk ▪ 1 cup flour
2 tablespoons baking cocoa ▪ 1 teaspoon baking powder
1/4 teaspoon salt ▪ 1/2 cup chopped walnuts
1/2 cup sugar ▪ 1/2 cup packed light brown sugar
1/4 cup baking cocoa ▪ 1 1/4 cups boiling water
Ice cream (optional)

Beat 3/4 cup sugar, butter and milk in mixer bowl until blended. Beat in mixture of flour, 2 tablespoons baking cocoa, baking powder and salt. Stir in walnuts. Spoon into greased 9x9-inch cake pan. Combine 1/2 cup sugar, brown sugar and 1/4 cup baking cocoa in bowl; mix well. Sprinkle over batter. Pour boiling water over top; do not stir. Bake at 350 degrees for 30 minutes. Cool for 10 minutes before serving. Spoon ice cream over top.
Yield: 9 servings.

Foolproof Microwave Fudge

1 can sweetened condensed milk
3 cups chocolate chips
1/8 teaspoon salt
1 cup chopped nuts
1 teaspoon vanilla extract

*Combine condensed milk, chocolate chips and salt in microwave-safe bowl.
Microwave for 1 minute; stir. Microwave for 45 seconds; stir until smooth. Stir
in nuts and vanilla. Spread in 9x13-inch greased pan. Chill for 2 hours; cut
into pieces. Yield: 36 pieces.*

Pecan Pralines

3 cups packed brown sugar
1/4 cup butter
1 cup whipping cream
1 1/2 cups broken pecans
1/8 teaspoon cinnamon

*Combine brown sugar, butter and whipping cream in saucepan. Cook over
low heat until sugar dissolves and mixture boils, stirring constantly.
Cook to 236 degrees on candy thermometer, stirring occasionally. Remove from
heat. Stir in pecans and cinnamon. Beat until thick and creamy. Drop by
tablespoonfuls 3 inches apart onto waxed paper. Let stand until firm.
Yield: 1 pound.*

Black Walnut Coconut Pound Cake

Black walnuts add a delightful tangy flavor to cakes, cookies, candy, salads, and pies.

2 cups sugar
1 cup vegetable oil
4 eggs, beaten
3 cups flour
1/2 teaspoon baking soda
1/2 teaspoon baking powder
1 cup buttermilk
1 cup chopped black walnuts
1 cup flaked coconut
2 teaspoons coconut extract
1/2 cup water
1 cup sugar
2 tablespoons butter
1 teaspoon coconut extract

Beat 2 cups sugar, oil and eggs in mixer bowl until blended. Add mixture of flour, baking soda and baking powder alternately with buttermilk, mixing well after each addition. Stir in black walnuts, coconut and 2 teaspoons coconut flavoring. Spoon into greased and floured bundt or tube pan. Bake at 325 degrees for 1 hour and 5 minutes or until cake tests done. Bring water, 1 cup sugar and butter to a boil in saucepan, stirring frequently. Boil for 5 minutes, stirring occasionally. Stir in 1 teaspoon coconut flavoring. Pour over hot cake in pan. Let stand for 4 to 8 hours. Heat cake in oven for several minutes to release side. Loosen cake from side of pan. Invert onto cake plate.
Yield: 16 servings.

Nuts

Peanut Butter Cake

2¼ cups flour
2 cups packed dark brown sugar
1 cup peanut butter ▪ ½ cup butter or margarine
1 teaspoon baking powder
½ teaspoon baking soda ▪ 1 teaspoon vanilla extract
3 eggs ▪ 1 cup milk
1 (12-ounce) package semisweet chocolate chips

Combine flour, brown sugar, peanut butter and butter in mixer bowl; mix well. Reserve 1 cup mixture. Add baking powder, baking soda, vanilla, eggs and milk to remaining mixture; mix until smooth. Pour into greased and floured 9x13-inch cake pan. Sprinkle with reserved peanut butter mixture. Sprinkle with chocolate chips. Bake at 350 degrees for 30 to 35 minutes or until knife inserted in center comes out clean.
Yield: 15 servings.

Turtle Cake

½ cup baking cocoa
1 cup boiling water ▪ ½ cup butter, softened
1¼ cups sugar ▪ ½ cup sour milk
1½ teaspoons baking soda ▪ 2 cups flour
1½ teaspoons vanilla extract ▪ 2 eggs
1 (14-ounce) can sweetened condensed milk
1 (14-ounce) package caramels
1 to 2 cups chocolate chips ▪ 1 cup chopped pecans

Dissolve baking cocoa in boiling water in bowl; mix well. Stir in butter and sugar until blended. Add mixture of sour milk and baking soda; mix well. Stir in flour, vanilla and eggs. Spoon ½ of batter into buttered 9x13-inch cake pan. Bake at 350 degrees for 15 minutes. Remove to wire rack to cool. Combine condensed milk and caramels in saucepan. Cook until smooth, stirring constantly. Spread evenly over baked layer. Sprinkle with chocolate chips and pecans. Top with remaining batter. Bake for 15 to 20 minutes longer or until cake tests done. May substitute 1 prepared package German chocolate cake mix for first 9 ingredients. May substitute walnuts for pecans.
Yield: 15 servings.

Macadamia Bar Cookies

1/2 cup butter, softened
1/4 cup confectioners' sugar
1 cup plus 2 tablespoons flour
2 eggs, lightly beaten
1 teaspoon vanilla extract
1 cup packed light brown sugar
2 tablespoons flour
1/2 teaspoon salt
1 cup flaked coconut
3/4 cup broken macadamia nuts

Cream butter and confectioners' sugar in bowl until light and fluffy. Stir in 1 cup plus 2 tablespoons flour. Pat into 9x9-inch baking pan. Bake at 325 degrees for 15 minutes or until light brown. Combine eggs and vanilla in bowl. Add brown sugar gradually. Add 2 tablespoons flour, salt, coconut and nuts; mix well. Pour over baked layer. Bake for 20 minutes or until toothpick inserted in center comes out clean. Cool. Cut into bars.
Yield: 9 servings.

Peanut Pie

1 cup sugar
1/2 teaspoon salt
1 cup creamy peanut butter
1/2 cup dark corn syrup
3 eggs
1 cup dry-roasted peanuts
1 unbaked (9-inch) pie shell
1 cup semisweet chocolate chips
2 tablespoons butter-flavor shortening

Cream first 3 ingredients in bowl until fluffy. Add corn syrup and eggs. Stir in peanuts. Pour into pie shell. Cover loosely with foil. Bake at 375 degrees for 30 minutes. Remove foil. Bake for 10 minutes longer or until crust is golden brown. Cool completely. Melt chocolate chips and shortening in double boiler. Spread over filling. Cool completely. Chill.
Yield: 16 servings.

Index